HANDPAINTING
YOUR *furniture*

HANDPAINTING YOUR *furniture*

Kerry Trout

NORTH LIGHT BOOKS
CINCINNATI, OHIO

www.nlbooks.com

ACKNOWLEDGEMENTS

I would like to thank my husband Tom, who has enriched my life and made all things possible. I thank him for his stoic patience and love. My heartfelt gratitude to my Dad for his selfless generosity and ardent support. Kudos to Amy, Kathy and Beth for their constant encouragement.

Much appreciation to Caroline Cave, Shannon Houk and Bob Houser. I would also like to thank my editors Kathy Kipp, Heather Dakota and photographer, Christine Polomsky. A special thank you goes to Sherry Bleier, who opened her store to a camera crew and endured several days of lights, cables and equipment in order to produce the photography on these pages. Without her hospitality and cooperation, this book would not have been possible.

FURNITURE PHOTOGRAPHED AT DÉJÀ VU ANTIQUES & COLLECTIBLES, BROWNSBURG, INDIANA

Other fine North Light Books are available from your local bookstore, art supply store or direct from the publisher.

04 03 02 01 00   5 4 3 2 1

Library of Congress Cataloging-in-Publication Data

Trout, Kerry
        Handpainting Your Furniture / Kerry Trout.
        p.   cm.
        ISBN 1-58180-014-2 (pb.: alk. paper). — ISBN 0-89134-980-4 (pb.: alk. paper)
        Furniture painting I. Title.
TT199.4 . T76 2000
745.7'23—dc21

Editors: Heather Dakota , Kathy Kipp and Nicole Hoch
Production Coordinator: Emily Gross
Designer: Stephanie Strang
Production Artist: Kathy Gardner
Photographer: Christine Polomsky

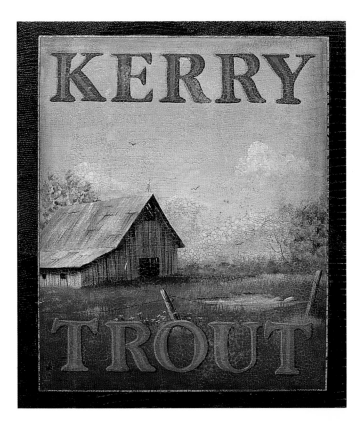

Kerry's been drawing and painting since childhood with much encouragement from her mother who was also an artist. She studied commercial art in college which lead her to a career in Graphic Arts. In her off hours, she taught herself to draw pastel portraits. This led her to be commissioned by Charlotte Motor Speedway where she drew portraits of the top NASCAR drivers.

Several years ago, Kerry began painting small items for a booth in a craft mall. When her company downsized, she found herself unemployed, but was encouraged by her husband to pursue painting full time. The one craft booth soon grew to five, keeping her very busy. However, it wasn't until she found a cabinet at a flea market and painted her first bunny hutch, which sold immediately, that she knew she had something special. She took her pieces to Déjà Vu Antiques to put them on consignment, but the owner bought them outright.

Kerry is also a member of the Society of Decorative Painters and a Helping Artist for DecoArt. Kerry was born in Indiana, but grew up in North Carolina. After 23 years, she realized that living in one place doesn't necessarily make it home, so she moved back to Indiana where she now resides.

dedication

In memory of Mom,

whose love of painting

was passed on to me.

PROJECT

1

page 26

Child's Rocker
with Violets

PROJECT

2

page 34

Botanical
Cupboard

PROJECT

5

page 72

Garden Shed
Cabinet

PROJECT

6

page 88

Marble-Topped
Bird Table

Table of Contents

furniture painting has seen many phases. Our pioneer ancestors, whose dwellings we assume were dark and drab, probably had, to the contrary, quite colorful surroundings. But decorating was expensive. A gallon of paint was not something they could pick up at the corner hardware store, because, quite frankly, neither one existed! An artisan would provide the service to those who could afford it, and because of that, painted furniture became a status symbol of the well-to-do. The artisan would make his rounds through the towns and countryside, painting tables, benches, hutches and chests in rich hues of red, green, yellow or blue milk paint that he mixed on site from powders. By 1820, paint became cheaper due to mass production. More colors were available than homeowners had ever had before, and as a result, homes became gaudy with color.

Later, the Victorian era reflected an abundance of highly polished oaks and mahoganys. From buffets to chiffonniers, the Victorians revered everything ornate and ostentatious. Paint was no longer at a premium, and if anything was painted, it was more likely to be the porch swing or picket fence.

Throughout the century, those old heirlooms were stripped and painted, and stripped and painted again, depending on what look was in vogue. Not too long ago we were limited to styles that were dictated by the furniture designers' lackluster imaginations—Mediterranean, contemporary or Early American. But today, absolutely anything goes. No longer are there strict rules to follow in home decorating. Mix all the styles of the past century in one room and we call it "eclectic"—the interior designer's latest catch word. But eclectic is a good thing, for it's my philosophy that as long as we surround ourselves with the things we love, we are happy.

Painted furniture has become a big part of today's decorating style. It can be a unique and beautiful objet d'art, serve as the focal point of a room, and sometimes even tell a story—yet remain as functional as it is fun to look at. I hope the information and projects in this book will inspire you to pick up a paintbrush and transform that ugly, plain piece of furniture (we all have one) into your own personal masterpiece.

Kerry Trout

What to Paint

So you've flipped through the pages of this book and you've been inspired to paint something. Great! Now it's time to start sifting around in the basement, garage and attic for a good project piece. Once you find it, make sure it's a piece that would only be enhanced by painting. Many antique pieces need to keep their original finish or patina in order to retain their value. As much as I love to transform an old piece, I won't put latex paint over a beautiful, 100-year-old oak finish! People have walked into my home and are quite surprised it isn't filled with my painted furniture. That's because most of the pieces I have are heirlooms that I wouldn't dream of painting. As much as I want you to try one of my projects, please think twice before painting your great-grandfather's rolltop desk! Also, this doesn't apply to wood finishes alone. Never paint over the original paint of an antique piece. Even if it's chipping or peeling, it can be stabilized by a professional to prevent further deterioration. Old paint finishes, although worn and unsightly, are historic documents that need to be treated as such.

There is a myriad of bargain furniture at secondhand stores, yard sales, auctions and flea markets. Don't shop for a nice-looking finish—remember, you'll be painting over it. But don't buy junk, either. You don't want to invest your time in something that's going to fall apart, so make sure it's sound. This doesn't mean to pass up a piece with missing knobs or drawers that stick. These flaws are easily fixed. Screws can be replaced and holes can be patched. So overlook the imperfections and dwell more on the style and overall sturdiness of the furniture.

A friendly word of advice: If the item you choose to paint has come out of a basement, garage or even a secondhand store, wash it off before you bring it into your house or work area. This includes the underside. There is bound to be a spiderweb under there and you don't want any surprises inside your home (trust me on this one!). You should wash the piece even if you plan on stripping it. I use a commercial oil soap diluted with water. This will remove any oils, dirt and grime. Rinse well, but don't soak the piece with water. Dry with paper towels immediately.

The availability of unfinished furniture is on the rise, partly due to the popularity of painted furniture. More and more, people are finding out they can paint for themselves what the designer stores are selling for hundreds of dollars. Unfinished furniture stores have a large array of country and traditional pieces, from jelly cabinets to armoires. Don't expect bargain prices at these outlets, however, as much as the trend has risen, so have the prices. The advantage of choosing unfinished furniture is that you are going to get a good quality piece, and you won't have to do any stripping or repair work before you start your painting. You also have a much better chance of finding the exact piece you want, and if you don't, they can probably order it for you.

Patterns in this Book

All finished projects in this book are merely examples of how to utilize the designs on them. It is unlikely that the piece you end up painting is going to be the exact same model of furniture as pictured. The patterns I have included for each project have been printed as large as space allows. The area you want to paint may be larger than what is actually shown in the pictures. Therefore, you'll need to enlarge the pattern. There are several ways of doing this.

ENLARGING PROJECTOR

This is a fast and easy way to enlarge a pattern or design and transfer it at the same time. Most projectors work in a similar way. They are designed specifically for enlarging images and work well, providing you use them in a very dark room. The image you want to enlarge is placed on a flat surface and the projector is placed on top of it. The projector allows you to adjust the size of the image it projects, so you can aim the projected image right onto your painting surface. Enlarging projectors are available through mail order and some craft and fine art supply stores. Depending on the model, the prices can range between $29 to $180.

COMPUTER SCANNER

Sometimes I can't wait until dark to use my projector, so I scan my pattern into my computer and print it out at the size I need. The image sometimes is too big to fit on an 8½ x 11-inch sheet of paper, so all I have to do is tape the sheets together. Then I use that as my pattern and put my graphite paper behind it. It's a method I use often and can work well for you if you have a computer, scanner and printer.

COPY MACHINE

You may also choose to go to the copy center and enlarge the pattern on a copy machine. You probably cannot get an undistorted copy if you lay this whole book on the copier, so I suggest tracing the pattern from the book first. To do this, lay a piece of tracing paper over the pattern and secure it on two sides with a small piece of painter's tape. Carefully trace over the pattern using a black marker. Now measure the height and width of the area you will be transferring your design to. Write this measurement in the corner of your traced pattern and take it to your local copy center to enlarge or reduce it. Many artists alter the size of their patterns this way, and the clerks at the copy centers are very adept at getting the exact size you need. However, to ensure that the pattern is going to turn out the right size, the clerk must know the size of the area it will be painted on, so be sure to write down those measurements. Don't forget to allow for a margin—in other words, make sure your image doesn't go clear to the edge of the painting surface if that isn't what you intend.

GRID METHOD

You can scale the pattern yourself using the grid method. Let's say you need the pattern to be twice its size to fit your painting surface. First, with a ruler and pencil, mark off 1-inch increments at the edges of the page.

> *hint* If you choose not to mark in this book, use a sheet of clear acetate and a fine-tipped permanent black marker.

Connect the marks with the ruler so that you have a grid of 1-inch squares. On your painting surface, mark off a grid in the same manner, but make the lines 2 inches apart. Be sure to make your lines very light, so they are easy to erase. Copy every line of the pattern that is in each 1-inch square on the grid into its corresponding 2-inch square on your painting surface. The result will be a 200% copy of the pattern. If you want the pattern only 1½ times its size, then you would make your grid marks 1½ inches wide; to make the pattern 3 times its size, grid squares would be 3 inches wide, and so on.

Supplies

Nothing is more frustrating than being in the middle of a project and needing a tool you don't have. Just as a mechanic has all his tools within reach, so should you. Don't let the list below intimidate you. You will already have some of the supplies on hand. If this is your first painting project, then you will need to stock up on the basic supplies. Keep in mind that every project shown in this book does not require every tool listed below. So read the project directions before spending money on something you may not need. The paints required to complete each project are listed in the beginning of the chapter.

PREPPING SUPPLIES

It is very important to properly prepare your furniture before painting it. These supplies will help you protect the wonderful painting you'll be adding, making your masterpiece a family heirloom.

- Drop cloth
- Small blocks of scrap wood or four bricks
- Sanding sponge
- Tack cloth
- Shellac or oil-based primer

MISCELLANEOUS PAINTING SUPPLIES

These miscellaneous supplies will make your work a lot easier and cleaner.

- 1-inch natural bristle brush
- 2-inch sponge brush
- White chalk pencil
- White and black transfer paper
- Tracing paper
- Paper towels
- Sea sponge
- Waxed paper
- Plastic wrap
- Latex gloves
- Painter's tape (low tack)
- Scotch Brand Magic tape
- X-Acto knife
- Tape measure
- T-square
- Straightedge
- Permanent black marker
- Water basin
- Lint-free rags
- Wax Candle

PALETTE

If you're a seasoned painter, you've probably tried all the different types of palettes available. There are palettes that promise to keep acrylic paints fresh for weeks, and other palettes are plastic or metal trays with shallow paint cups, but these palettes require regular cleaning. Paper palettes come in tablets with sheets you tear off as needed. All of the above, in my opinion, either limit you or are expensive, or both. When you paint furniture, you'll usually need a large amount of color on your palette at one time. I find a Styrofoam plate to be the best palette. The Styrofoam plates are white, so when you're mixing a wash, there is no color distortion from the plate. They are inexpensive, so you can simply toss them away when you need a clean palette. When you want to save the paint on your palette, invert another plate over it, weight it down with a magazine, and your paint will stay fresh over night.

ANTIQUING AND FAUX FINISHING SUPPLIES

These tools give a nice aged appearance, even if you're working with a brand-new piece of furniture.

- Awl
- Rock
- Wood stain
- Wire brush
- Drop cloth
- Sponge brushes
- Neutral Wall Glaze
- Wood Stain
- Sanding sponge
- Latex gloves
- Styrofoam plate

BRUSHES

Any artist will tell you that nothing contributes more to a successful painting than good quality brushes. With the popularity of decorative painting growing, artists have demanded affordable quality tools, and many companies offer a full line of brushes that stand up to acrylic and latex paints. If the ones you have lose bristles as you paint, throw them away and buy the best brushes you can afford.

The projects in this book call for a variety of brush types and sizes. For laying down paint onto large areas, you'll need a couple of good, natural bristle brushes, 1 inch and 3 inches in width. Disposable sponge brushes may be used, also. They are inexpensive, easy to clean, and will last through several projects.

For detail work, it is essential that you use the appropriate brush to achieve the best results or to create a certain look. The following is a list of artists' brushes used for the projects in this book. The painting instructions for each project indicate the type of brush and size required.

- $1/4$", $1/2$", 1" flat shader
- nos. 0, 2 round
- nos. 5/0, 2 script liner
- $1/4$" cat's tongue (or filbert)
- $1/4$" rake brush
- $1/2$" dagger striper
- no. 2 or 3, $1/4$" mop brush
- no. 2 fan brush
- $1/2$" deer foot stippler

Specialty Brushes

For faux finishes, use the appropriate brush to create a certain look. The painting instructions for each project indicate the type of specialty brush required.

• Sponge brushes in a variety of sizes
• Hake brush
• Mop Brush
• Oil painting brushes
• Brush cleaner

Care and Cleaning of Brushes

If you invest in a good set of artists' brushes, it only makes sense to take care of them. Acrylic paint can be especially hard on the bristles, so extra care is needed to keep your brushes like new.

Be sure to wash the sizing out of the brush with mild soap and warm water before using the brush. Bending the bristles to break their stiffness may damage them.

hint *Always start a painting project with fresh water. A large container, such as a clean plastic pail, is better than a small cup—you won't have to change the water as often. The sediments in dirty water will settle back onto the bristles and can shorten the life of your brush and can muddy your colors, especially white.*

It is important to avoid getting paint in the ferrule. It is next to impossible to remove paint once it dries in there. The dried paint will separate the bristles at the base resulting in a tunnel effect where the bristles flare out. A brush in this condition cannot perform properly, and painting becomes a struggle.

When rinsing paint from your brush, don't mash it on the bottom of the basin or scrape the bristles on a built-in "scrubber" to remove paint. This will damage the bristles and distort the brush's form. Instead, tap your brush gently under water against the side of the basin until no more paint comes out.

Never leave brushes standing in water! It will ruin the ends of the bristles, and eventually allow water to soak into the handle of the brush, causing the enamel coating on the handle to crack and peel off.

When painting is done for the day, wash your brushes in warm, soapy water. Follow up with a brush cleaner. There are several cleaners on the market to choose from. I prefer The Masters Brush Cleaner and Preserver. Be sure to reshape the bristles and lay the brushes flat to dry.

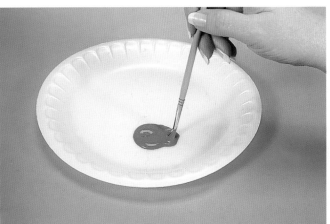

PAINTS

I saw a lady admiring a dresser recently and she asked me what type of paint I used on it, alkyds or oils. I told her I use only acrylics and latex enamels. Her face fell in disappointment as she replied, "Oh. I heard that serious furniture painters use only alkyds or oils." With as much going for them as acrylic paints have, why wouldn't artists choose them over oil-based paints? Acrylic paints dry in far less time than oil paints and they are water-soluble. This means your cleanup consists of soap and water, as opposed to mineral spirits, turpentine, paint thinner or other toxic solvents, so it is much safer for you and the environment. The base paintings for the projects in this book are painted with American Accents® by Rust-Oleum latex enamels, and the decorative painting was done with DecoArt Americana acrylic paints. The exact colors needed are provided in the beginning of each project.

Mediums

Mediums are designed to lengthen the drying time of your acrylics, create wonderful faux finishes, and float color effortlessly.

Prepare Your Surface

Whether you are starting with an old hutch or a new, unfinished desk, the surface must be prepared properly. Don't be so eager to paint that you skip the preparation. Doing so can cause disappointing, and sometimes disastrous, results.

If the piece you're going to paint has an old varnish or many layers of old, chipping paint, it should be removed. You may consider a commercial home furniture stripping kit. If choosing this method, read the label carefully. Also, some of these strippers eat through certain plastics, so make sure your drop cloth is suitable.

Professional furniture strippers can save you the mess and time, but they can be very pricey. However, all previously finished pieces need not be stripped. The whole idea is to create a rougher surface that the new paint can adhere to, and that is achieved by either stripping or sanding.

SAND THE SURFACE

Sanding is an essential part of preparation and must be done correctly to avoid damaging the wood surface. If at all possible, sand outdoors. You'll avoid having dust settle on everything and you won't be inhaling the wood dust or paint particles that may contain lead. If you must sand indoors, wear a protective mask that covers both the mouth and nose. Remove all the drawers, drawer pulls, knobs and hardware. Inspect them for any protruding nail heads or holes. Re-sink any nails and fill holes with a commercial wood filler. Allow the wood filler to dry completely before sanding.

I find the new sanding sponges just as good as, if not better than, ordinary sandpaper. They are easier to hold and last longer, plus they are flexible and can lend themselves to the contour of the surface you are sanding. Most sponges are available in various grit weights—heavy to fine—so pick the one that would be right for the job you are doing. Don't use a heavy grit if you don't have to; it can easily scratch the wood surface. If you are working on unfinished furniture, a heavy grit is not needed at all. Always sand in the direction of the wood grain. If

you don't, you can create scratches on the surface that will show through paint. If you are sanding a previously painted surface and cannot tell the direction of the grain, sand along the longest plane. When "roughing up" old paint, it is not necessary to sand down to the bare wood, but sand enough to remove any shine from the old surface.

When sanding is complete, remove all dust. This is important, as the tiniest speck of dust can appear much larger under a coat of paint. I keep a handheld vacuum nearby for this. Or you

can use a dampened (not wet) cotton cloth. Don't be tempted to blow the sawdust away. It will only settle back on your surface and everything else in your workroom. You can use a small, old paintbrush to remove dust from corners. When the visible dust is removed, go over the entire piece with a tack cloth. It is essential for removing the dust you can't see. To get the most mileage from a tack cloth, don't unfold it when you take it from the package. Use one side of it until it has lost its adhesion, then turn it over and use the other side. Store the tack cloth in an airtight container for future use.

PRIME THE SURFACE

Any surface must be primed before the application of your base coat. Raw wood acts like a sponge and will soak up the first coat of paint. A primer will prevent this. If you are working on a new, unfinished piece, it is probably made of pine and contains knots that will ooze tannin, a sticky, saplike substance, if it is not properly sealed. If you don't prime the knots, dark rings will rise to the surface of your furniture through your wonderful painting. Prime unfinished wood with a good shellac, such as Zinsser Bulls Eye. Apply with a bristle brush just as you would paint, and follow the manufacturer's directions. Be sure to have adequate ventilation.

> *hint* Do not use a sponge brush to apply shellac. Agents in the shellac will react with the synthetic sponge and it will disintegrate. Allow the primer to dry for at least six hours. Shellac will raise the grain of the wood, so lightly sand the entire piece again and use the tack cloth to remove dust.

If your furniture looks to have had a cherry or mahogany finish, it may look pinkish now that the varnish has been removed. You should assume the finish contains aniline dye. Early Victorian wood stains contained aniline dye that helped create those deep, reddish wood tones, and it can be disastrous under a coat of paint. Painting over metallic gold paint can cause the same problem. So keep in mind that an oil-based pigment may give you problems if you apply water-based latex on top of it. If in doubt as to whether or not the old surface is oil-based, prime it. An oil-based pigmented primer, such as Kilz, or aluminum-based paint will prevent the old surface from rearing its ugly head. Check the label on the can to be sure the product blocks aniline dyes.

BASECOAT THE SURFACE

Basecoating refers to the application of latex enamel that is used to paint the furniture. I use American Accents® by Rust-Oleum, an excellent interior/exterior paint for most paintable surfaces. Rust-Oleum has grouped their American Accents line into five color collections: Heritage, Garden, Tapestry, Classic and Country Home. Within each color collection you can select shades that work together no matter how they are combined. However, you are by no means restricted to these color collections. This grouping is really for taking the guesswork out of color-combining. I have used Taupe and Ivory Silk—colors from two different collections—and they work beautifully. If you like the color, then that's all that matters!

If you prefer your project to look as much like the picture as possible, you'll find the one-quart cans of American Accents® line wherever Rust-Oleum paints are sold. They offer about forty colors that are popular in today's home decorating. One

quart of paint will be more than enough to cover even the largest armoire.

You don't necessarily have to stick to the colors I used on the projects, and you're not limited to the colors you find on the store shelf. In fact, you can take in a wallpaper sample or fabric swatch and your paint dealer can quickly computer match any color. But if you plan on custom-mixing your color, you will find it less expensive to buy a gallon.

Paint that has been sitting for any period of time separates and needs to be thoroughly mixed. Ask for a paint stir stick, and a paint can opener. These two items are necessities and many dealers give them away when you purchase paint.

After the surface of your furniture has been properly sanded and primed, you're ready to apply your basecoat. Spread out a clean drop cloth or newspaper. If you must use the same drop cloth, make sure there is no sanding dust left on it.

I like to use blocks under the feet or bottom edge of whatever I'm painting. Small scraps of wood or four bricks will do fine. Wrapped in waxed paper, they become buffers between the furniture and the drop cloth that paint won't stick to. You don't want the legs or bottom of the piece to dry to the drop cloth or newspaper.

Stir your paint and pour a good portion onto a Styrofoam plate, a sturdy plastic bowl or similar container. Dipping your brush in and out of the original will contaminate the unused paint.

hint To prevent paint from collecting inside the rim of the can, use a large nail and hammer to make three or four holes in the bottom of the rim. Any paint collected in there will drip back down into the can.

If you plan to paint the inside of your project piece, do that first. This includes drawers and the door backs you may have removed before sanding. Always start at the top and paint down. Use a good quality bristle brush or sponge brush and apply light, even strokes. Always paint in the direction of the grain, or along the longest plane. Avoid applying heavy coats, as this will only cause runs and extended drying time. Pick out any foreign particles while the paint is wet.

When the first coat is completely dry, lightly sand it to remove the raised grain. I use a Teflon scrubbing pad for this sanding step—it doesn't leave the gritty residue like a sanding sponge. Remove the dust with a tack cloth. Wait two to four hours before applying the second coat, but re-coat within forty-eight hours. Don't paint in direct sunlight, as this causes the paint to dry too fast. Best results are achieved indoors with adequate ventilation (always follow precautions printed on the product label). Although most latex enamels are dry to the touch in a couple of hours, there is a "curing" time that paint requires before the furniture can be used. In other words, the paint may look and feel dry, but it also has to harden. I ask my clients to wait thirty days before setting anything heavy—like a lamp or vase—on the surface. If this is not possible, put a sheet of waxed paper between the item and the surface. Paint that has not had time to cure, especially in high humidity, is still soft and can actually stick to the bottom of whatever you set on top of it.

MASKING OFF AN AREA

If any area, such as trim work, is to be a different color, you can mask it off to avoid getting paint on the adjacent surface. This can be done only after the surface you want to protect has dried thoroughly, at least twenty-four hours. Use low-tack painter's tape. Most paint dealers will have several types to choose from. Painter's tape is more expensive than ordinary masking tape, but it is well worth it. Common masking tape is textured, allowing paint to seep under its edges. Its adhesion is too strong, and it could pull up paint when you remove it. When masking off an area, make sure all edges of the tape are down securely before applying paint. Remove the tape before the paint is completely dry. I usually wait about thirty to forty-five minutes. The time will depend on the humidity where you live.

AGING AND ANTIQUING

I antique and distress just about everything I do. I like the time-worn look it gives to a new piece of furniture. Many of the items I paint are new country reproductions, and it's a challenge to see how old I can make them look. Also, there are different degrees of antiquing, and you may find one or the other suits your taste or your decor best.

Rock 'n' Roll Method

This method creates a gently worn look and adds instant age to your freshly painted furniture. The process is done after all other painting is completely dried. I wait a full twenty-four hours before antiquing. Listed below are the supplies you'll need to successfully age your painted furniture with this method:

• Neutral Wall Glaze
• Carver Tripp® Safe and Simple™ Wood Stain (Special Walnut)
• Large, rough rock, approx. 4 to 5 lbs.
• Styrofoam plate
• 2- to 3-inch sponge brush
• Clean, lint-free rag or paper towels
• Sanding sponge
• Tack cloth

When you look at a truly old piece of furniture, you will see worn edges and rounded corners, and little nicks and dents that have occurred over the years. If you want your new item to look just as old, then you will need to create the imperfections yourself. This is done by what I like to call my Rock 'n' Roll technique.

Turn the surface that you will be working on horizontally. Wax the edges of the piece with a candle, the paint will come off easier in the sanding step. Then, gently roll your rock over the surface. Don't worry if you don't see much happening, the dents and knicks left by the rock will show up after the antiquing process. Do this on any surface that would normally collect wear marks, and at the end of all table and chair legs.

Next, using the sanding block, sand any edges and outside corners where paint would naturally wear off through years of use. Don't be timid—sand down to the wood. And if you remembered to wax the edges, the paint will come off easier. Sharp corners should be rounded slightly. Sand down the area around any knobs or drawer pulls that would normally be worn down by years of hand contact. If the knobs are wood, don't forget to make them time-worn, too. Remove all sanding dust with a tack cloth. If you removed any doors and hardware at the beginning of your project, replace them before the next step.

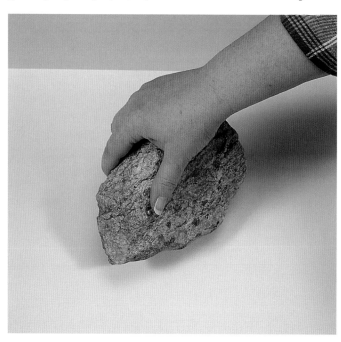

Antique the Wood

In a shallow plastic container or Styrofoam plate, mix two parts Neutral Wall Glaze to one part water-based wood stain. Starting at the top of your piece, brush the antiquing mixture around the edges, making sure the mixture gets into the crevices of any molding and ornate carvings. Then brush it thinly across the rest of the surface. Using a clean rag, immediately wipe off the antiquing in circular motions until you achieve the desired aged effect. If you want a less antiqued look, use a dampened rag when removing the mixture.

Remove the Antiquing Stain

Antique one surface of your furniture at a time. Never let the antiquing mixture sit long enough on the surface to begin drying. Move around your piece, antiquing from the top down. Brush over any hardware, such as hinges. Hardware ages and discolors, too, and on very old pieces, dirt collects over the years around these parts, so when wiping the mixture off, allow some to remain around the edges of the hinges and knobs. The antiquing mixture should remain in any crevices, cracks, knicks and dents—don't try to remove it. Taking off too much of the antiquing will defeat the purpose. Anywhere you sanded down to bare wood also should have been darkened by the antiquing process. If, after you are done, you prefer an even heavier aged look, wait twenty-four hours before antiquing again.

Little Grape Table

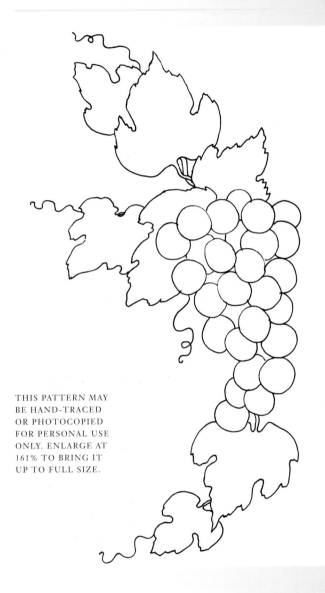

THIS PATTERN MAY
BE HAND-TRACED
OR PHOTOCOPIED
FOR PERSONAL USE
ONLY. ENLARGE AT
161% TO BRING IT
UP TO FULL SIZE.

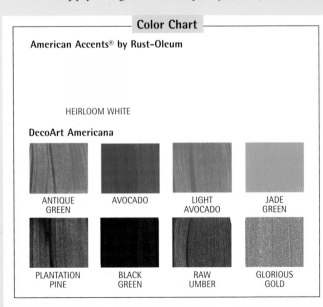

You're bound to find a little plant stand or table like this in your house or at a flea market, to which you can apply the great techniques you've just learned.

Miscellaneous Supplies:
- Neutral Wall Glaze
- Small sea sponge

Brushes:
- ¼", ½" flat shaders
- no. 1 round
- nos. 0 and 5/0 script liner
- ½" dagger striper
- Large mop brush or hake

Prepare the Surface

Prepare an old surface as described in *Prepare Your Surface*, p. 15. When your prepping is completed base-coat the surface with two coats of Heirloom White.

Color Chart

American Accents® by Rust-Oleum

HEIRLOOM WHITE

DecoArt Americana

ANTIQUE GREEN	AVOCADO	LIGHT AVOCADO	JADE GREEN
PLANTATION PINE	BLACK GREEN	RAW UMBER	GLORIOUS GOLD

Paint the Subtle Stucco

s t e p **1** · In a shallow container, mix thoroughly 2 parts Neutral Wall Glaze to 1 part Honey Brown.

s t e p **2** · Take a dry mop brush in the hand you normally paint with, and with the other hand, dip one side of a dampened sea sponge into the glaze mixture. Starting at the top of your furniture, lightly and randomly sponge the glaze mixture onto your surface. Work in a very small area at one time—about an 8-inch square; don't cover the entire surface.

s t e p **3** · With a light touch, immediately begin diffusing the glaze with the mop brush, making Xs and figure eights in the glaze. Leave no pattern in the glaze. If you see circles or a pattern forming or if your brush is leaving tracks in the glaze, you may have applied too much. Turn the sponge over and blot with the clean side to remove any excess. It is also important to keep the brush as dry as possible, because it will make tracks in the glaze when it becomes saturated. Rinse the brush when it becomes saturated, and squeeze as much water out of it as you can with a few paper towels. Then fluff the brush against a wad of paper towel to separate the bristles and continue working.

Let this layer of glaze dry approximately two hours. Save the leftover glaze.

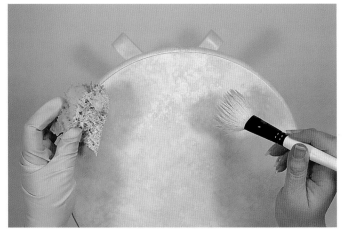

s t e p **4** · Mix 2 parts glaze with 1 part Heirloom White, and repeat the entire process on top of the first glaze mixture of Honey Brown to soften the effect.

s t e p **5** · Add a few random "cracks" and imperfections in the subtle stucco finish by loading your dagger striper with the Honey Brown glaze mixture and dragging it across the surface, twisting the brush as you drag. For realistic hairline cracks, dilute Raw Umber and use a no. 5/0 liner to apply very tiny "shaky" lines that stem from knobs or corners. Let this dry overnight before applying any decorative painting.

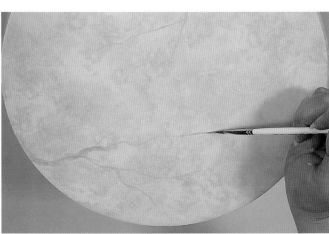

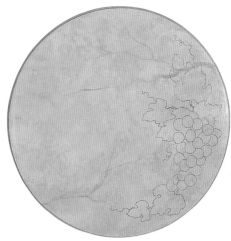

Transfer the pattern. Freehand a vine and a few leaves around the bottom of the table leg and feet.

Paint the Grape Leaves

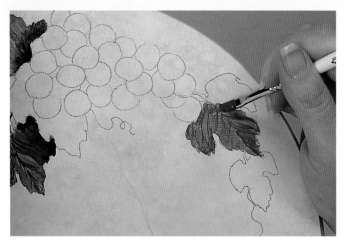

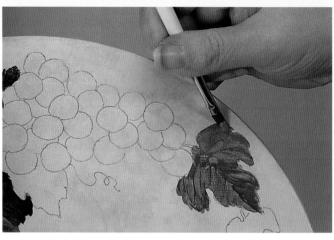

s t e p 1 · Dampen the leaves with clear water using a ¼-inch shader. Load the brush with Hauser Medium Green and run the chisel edge lightly down the center of the leaf. Put the chisel edge against the leaf's outline at the tip and pull the brush down to the center vein you just painted and halfway down the leaf. Your paint strokes should be translucent and your strokes visible.

s t e p 2 · With the dirty brush (don't rinse out the paint from step 1), pick up a bit of Antique Green and continue making strokes from the edge of the leaf to the center.

s t e p 3 · Rinse the brush and load it with Black Green, and continue around the base of the leaf. If the center vein looks irregular now, you can run the chisel edge of the brush along it to correct the line. If the water on the curled leaf has dried by this time, re-wet it and paint the inside Antique Green and the underside Black Green.

s t e p 4 · Paint the tendril and stem Antique Green and add shading with Black Green. You can use either a toothpick or a liner brush loaded with thinned Jade Green to create the veins in the leaves.

Paint the Grapes

step *1* · Add the shadows to the deepest gaps of the grape cluster.

step *2* · Basecoat the grapes with two coats of Avocado. Turn your work to make it easier to paint.

step *3* · Add highlights along the upper edge of each grape with a no. 6 shader loaded with Light Avocado. Pat-blend to erase hard lines.

step *4* · Shade the grapes on the lower edges in the same manner using the no. 6 shader loaded with Plantation Pine.

step *5* · Add the final highlight with a comma stroke of Jade Green using a no. 1 round brush.

step *6* · Define the grapes on the shaded edge with a no. 0 liner brush loaded with Light Avocado.

The Final Touches

step 1 · Mix the shadow color using DecoArt Burnt Umber, Prussian Blue, and Charcoal Grey and thin with water.

step 2 · Add the shadow on the right side of the grapes. This will give even more definition.

step 3 · The gold trim is drybrushed on the rim of the table using a dry ½-inch flat brush minimally loaded with Glorious Gold.

CREATE ANTIQUE MOSSING

step 1 · Mix 2 parts Avocado with 1 part Raw Umber, then add 3 parts Neutral Wall Glaze and mix well.

step 2 · Apply the mossing sparingly and randomly with a small sponge to seams and inside corners and around door knobs. (Use a small brush to get into corners and crevices.)

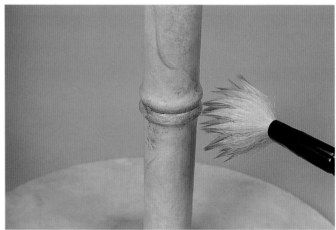

step 3 · Then immediately diffuse the paint with the dry mop brush, using the small figure eights and Xs mentioned earlier. All edges of the mossing should blend into transparency.

The completed tabletop

Detail of the completed tabletop

Detail of the table leg and bottom

The completed table

Child's Rocker with Violets

This rocker, although sound with years of life left, was quite an

eyesore and needed some sprucing up before it was fit for a little girl.

You can pick up small chairs and rockers at flea markets, yard sales

and unfinished furniture stores. This violet motif is a quick and easy

project that would be wonderful for a special little girl, or maybe you!

m a t e r i a l s

General Supplies:
- Transfer paper
- Styrofoam plate
- Paper towels
- Latex gloves
- Plastic wrap
- Neutral Wall Glaze
- X-Acto knife
- Ruler
- Compressed sponge
- Toothpicks
- Stylus
- Painter's tape (low tack)
- Water-based polyurethane

Brushes:
- ½"flat shader
- 5/0 liner brush
- ¼" filbert brush

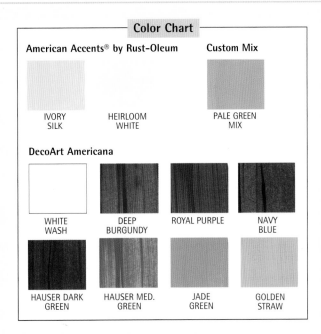

Color Chart

American Accents® by Rust-Oleum

IVORY SILK

HEIRLOOM WHITE

Custom Mix

PALE GREEN MIX

DecoArt Americana

WHITE WASH

DEEP BURGUNDY

ROYAL PURPLE

NAVY BLUE

HAUSER DARK GREEN

HAUSER MED. GREEN

JADE GREEN

GOLDEN STRAW

THESE PATTERNS MAY BE HAND-TRACED OR PHOTOCOPIED FOR PERSONAL USE ONLY.
ENLARGE AT 128% TO BRING THEM UP TO FULL SIZE.

Pounce with Plastic Wrap

Before

s t e p **1** · Basecoat the rocker with two coats of Ivory Silk. Mix 1 part Neutral Wall Glaze with 1 part Heirloom White on a Styrofoam plate. Put on gloves and tear off about four feet of plastic wrap, wadding it up into a ball, but don't have it too loose or it will be hard to handle. Dip one side of the wad into the glaze mixture and blot it on a paper towel to remove the excess paint. You don't want your plastic wrap to be dripping. Pounce all over the surface of the chair lightly and randomly, but allow plenty of the base coat to show through. Discard the plastic wrap.

s t e p **2** · Mix 1 part Ivory Silk with 1 part glaze. Apply over the surface as you did the first glaze, but don't completely cover the first layer. Let this dry completely, at least twenty-four hours.

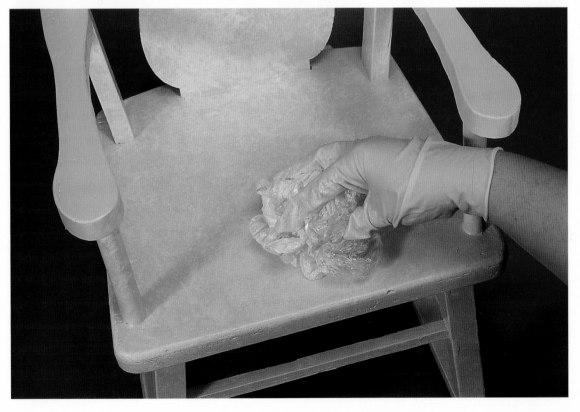

Add the Checkered Borders

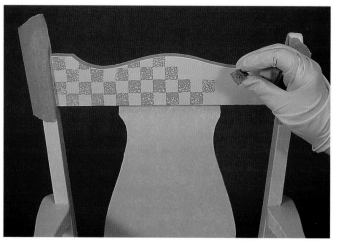

s t e p *1* · Mix 1 part Moss Green with 2 parts Heirloom White to make a Pale Green mix. Mask off any adjacent areas that your sponge shouldn't touch. Use an X-Acto knife and a ruler to cut a ¾-inch square from a compressed sponge. Wet the sponge to expand it and squeeze out the excess water. Dip the sponge into the Pale Green mix and blot it on a paper towel. Apply the checkerboard pattern to the back of the chair, starting in the middle against a straight edge. Put the sponge on the surface, tap it lightly with one finger and remove it. Move the sponge up diagonally so that the lower corner will meet the upper corner of the just-painted square. Apply and tap again. Continue making the checkerboard in this manner.

s t e p *2* · Now, apply the same effect to the runners and one single row around the seat edge. Rinse the sponge. Paint the arms with two coats of the Pale Green mix.

s t e p *3* · Lightly mark off a 2-inch margin from the top edge of the seat. Sponge a checkerboard border, just two rows deep, with Heirloom White. Start in one corner and work around. Let this dry. Transfer the violet pattern onto the chair back, then the seat. Use a single flower from the pattern to apply to one chair leg.

Paint the Leaves

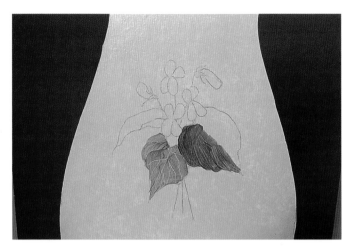

step 4 · Put Jade Green, Hauser Dark Green and Hauser Medium Green on your palette. Load a ½-inch flat shader with any of these colors and apply to the outer edge of a leaf, bringing the stroke in to the leaf's center.

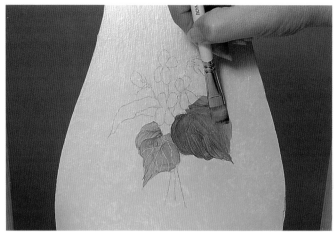

step 5 · Don't rinse your brush, but pull it through a different shade of green and wipe it back and forth on your palette to get a nice chisel edge. Paint the other side of the leaf as you did the first—from the edge into the center. Your leaves will be somewhat translucent, so don't try to paint a second coat on them or be concerned about "muddying" colors. These leaves look more natural when there are several color shades used. Since you will add the veins by dragging a toothpick through the wet paint, it is important that the leaf colors be applied quickly, but with a light touch. Use new toothpicks, if the point becomes flat.

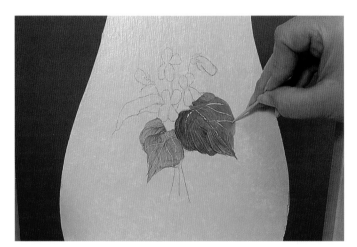

step 6 · As soon as you finish one leaf, immediately drag the tip of a toothpick from the base to the tip of the leaf. Then, make additional veins branch out from the center. The idea is to move the paint, so the base coat will show through. If you wait too long, the paint will dry and peel when you attempt to drag the toothpick through it.

step 7 · Add stems and tendrils with the liner brush loaded with a blend of greens from your palette.

Paint the Violets

s t e p **8** · Squeeze small amounts of Deep Burgundy, Royal Purple, Navy Blue and White Wash onto your palette. Load one side of your filbert brush with Royal Purple, and the other side with Navy Blue.

s t e p **9** · Dip just the tip into White Wash and apply the violet, pressing the end of the brush against the tip of the petal. Pull toward the center of the flower where you taper the stroke to a point. Your result should be a blend of purplish-blue tints with streaks of white. Don't go over the stroke once you've painted it. The petals are made with only one stroke and you don't want to blend or muddy the colors.

s t e p **10** · Paint another petal on the same flower in the same manner. Vary the shade slightly on individual flowers by using either more or less Royal Purple or Navy Blue, and add Deep Burgundy occasionally. Any variation is fine.

s t e p **11** · When the violets are dry, make three dip-dots in the center of each flower with a toothpick or stylus loaded with Golden Straw.

The Finished Chair

When the painting is completely dry, seal the violets with a thin coat of polyurethane. The rest of the chair does not need to be sealed, because the Rust-Oleum colors already have a sealer in them.

Seat, detail.

Leg, detail.

Rocker back, detail.

The completed rocker

Anthemis nobilis

Asperula odorata

Pachysandra

Carissa carpa

Botanical Cupboard

Visit just about any antique store and you can find an old jelly cupboard.

They are sought after by collectors and decorators for their nostalgic

charm and great age, but no longer are they just for Grandma's

homemade preserves. Today they can hold anything from linens

to CDs, and this reproduction, painted in neutral tones with delicate

botanicals, is a timeless design adaptable to any room in the house.

materials

General Supplies:
- Transfer paper
- Pencil
- Straight edge
- Paper towels
- Latex gloves
- Water-based polyurethane

Brushes:
- 1 and 2 inch sponge brushes
- $^1/_4$" flat shader
- nos. 000, 2 round
- nos. 5/0, 000 script liner

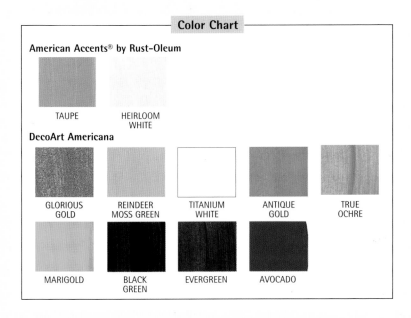

Color Chart

American Accents® by Rust-Oleum

TAUPE   HEIRLOOM WHITE

DecoArt Americana

GLORIOUS GOLD   REINDEER MOSS GREEN   TITANIUM WHITE   ANTIQUE GOLD   TRUE OCHRE

MARIGOLD   BLACK GREEN   EVERGREEN   AVOCADO

Prepare the Surface

Prepare the wood surface as instructed on page 15. Basecoat everything except the trim with two coats of Heirloom White. Paint the trim with Taupe. Transfer the Botanicals pattern onto the doors, omitting the veins of the leaves.

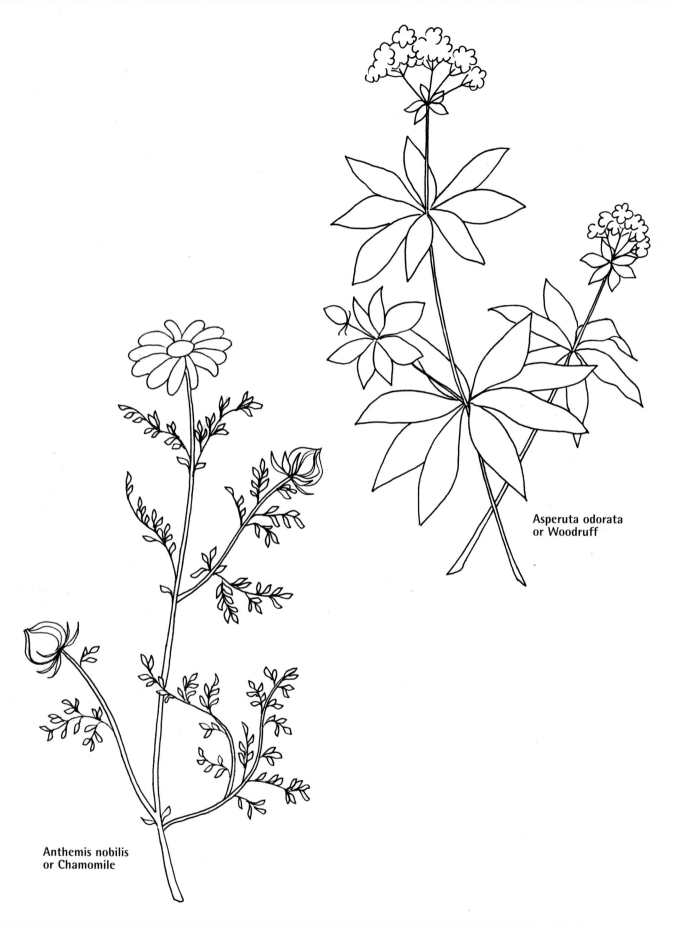

Asperuta odorata or Woodruff

Anthemis nobilis or Chamomile

THESE PATTERNS MAY BE HAND-TRACED OR PHOTOCOPIED FOR PERSONAL USE ONLY.
ENLARGE AT 133% TO BRING THEM UP TO FULL SIZE.

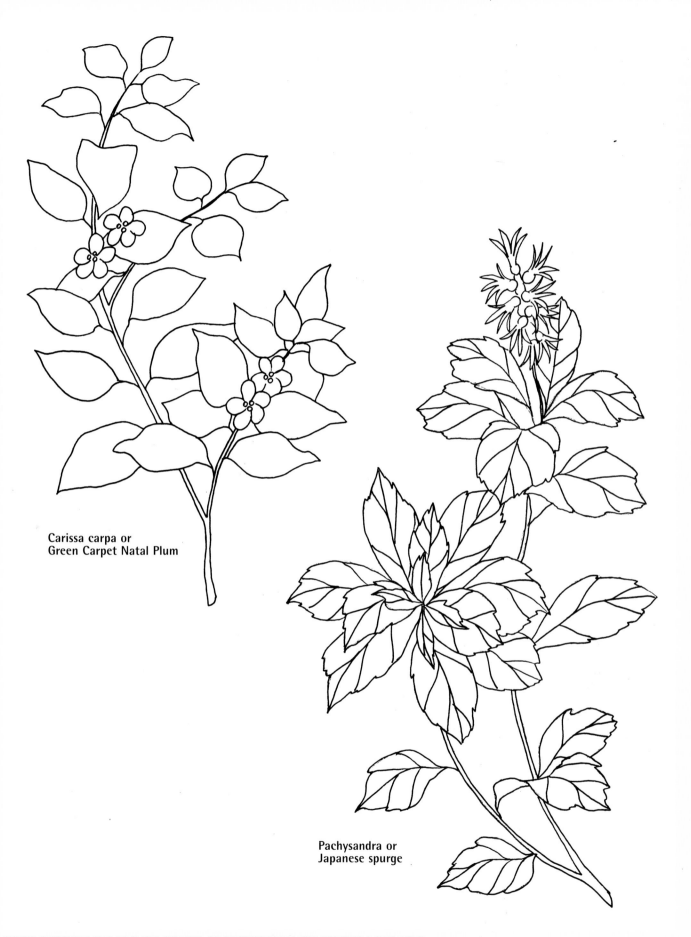

Carissa carpa or
Green Carpet Natal Plum

Pachysandra or
Japanese spurge

Anthemis nobilis (Chamomile)

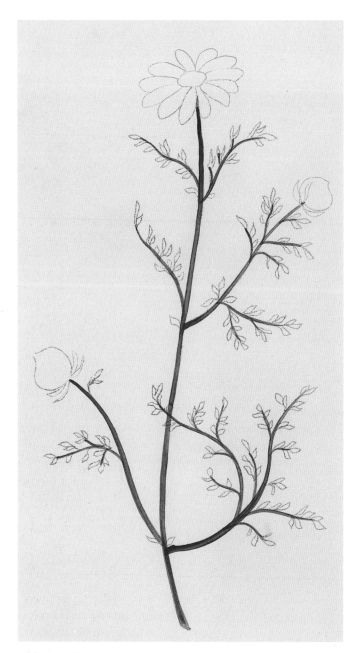

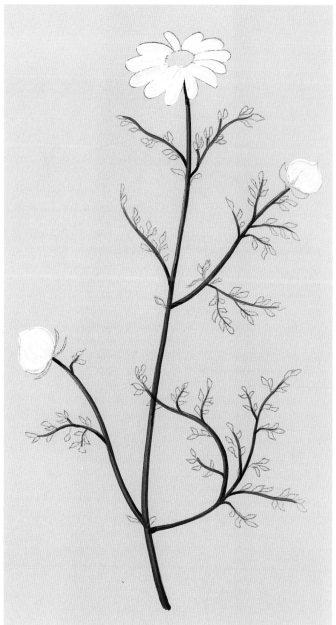

s t e p **1** · Thin Avocado to the consistency of ink. Paint the stem using a no. 5/0 script liner.

> *hint* *I find I have more control over a script liner when I pull the brush toward me during a long stroke. There's no rule that says your artwork must be right side up when painting. So if you'd be more comfortable turning your painting surface, do so.*

Since this is a vertical door panel, I place my brush just under the top bloom and pull it down, maintaining an even pressure until I get near the end of the stem. Then, I apply a bit more pressure, causing the bristles to spread out slightly, resulting in a wider end. The fluid consistency of the paint is important. It will allow you to finish a long stroke without interrupting the smooth flow.

s t e p **2** · Apply Evergreen to shade the right side and underneath areas of the stem with the same script liner. Use Black Green and a no. 000 script liner brush to add deep shadows at the base of the blooms, and at the base of the small stems branching out from the main one.

Apply Titanium White with a no. 2 round brush to the petals of the flower and the buds. Using a round brush will create ridges on the edges of your paint stroke, but don't smooth them out. Painting petals and foliage with a round brush adds texture to the Chamomile petals.

s t e p **3** · When the petals are dry, re-apply white to the petals on the left side of the flower. This will intensify and brighten the white, while serving as a highlight. The rest of the petals are fine with only one coat. Do the same for the buds, adding more Titanium White to the left side.

Apply a thin line of highlight to the stems with Reindeer Moss Green just opposite where you painted shadows. Use the no. 000 script liner, making sure the paint is very thin and the brush is fully loaded. If you find that you applied it too watery, wait until it dries and go over the stroke with slightly thicker paint. Use the same liner to add shading to the bloom and buds with Reindeer Moss Green. Bring a few arched strokes from the base of each bud to the tip. This will suggest the shadow of unopened petals. On the open bloom, shade the outer edges of the petals and about three-quarters of the way down the center of a few petals. Apply this same color around the base of the bloom's center, and bring a few short, pointed strokes from the center out and down the sides of a few petals to help separate the petals. Paint the center Marigold.

s t e p **4** · Thin Avocado just enough to load a no. 000 round brush without it "globbing" on the bristles. Each individual leaf is one little stroke. To do this, hold your brush at an angle—much like you would a pencil—and press the bristles down gently as you pull slightly, lifting the brush as you pull. The pointed bristles will leave a tiny tail on your stroke when done correctly. Make sure your stroke begins at the stem. The tail of the stroke will be the tip of the leaf. Use straight Reindeer Moss Green on the leaves at the tip of each stem. Vary the colors of the leaves as much as you want, but maintain the same size.

Paint the sepals at the base of each bud Avocado, and shade with Black Green. Shade the right side center with True Ochre and add a touch of highlight by mixing a bit of White with Marigold. Be careful not to make the highlight too white suggesting a reflection. This would not occur on this flower. Darken a tiny bit of Reindeer Moss Green with Avocado, and add a few dots around the base of the bloom's center.

Asperuta odorata (Woodruff)

s t e p **1** · Thin Avocado until it's the consistency of ink. Apply it with a ¼-inch flat shader, starting at the tip of the larger leaves and ending the stroke at the stem. Your stroke marks should be visible to make it look natural. Paint the smaller leaves with a no. 2 round brush.

s t e p **2** · Apply Evergreen to each leaf near the stem, and where one leaf is shadowed by another. Apply this color sparingly to the tips of a few leaves and the edges of others to create dimension. Smooth out any hard lines with a damp brush. Thin the color until watery, and use a no. 000 round brush to run a center vein.

s t e p **3** · Deepen the darkest areas of the shadows with Black Green. Apply it in the shadow of the bottom leaf and directly against the upper leaf edge. This will actually "lift" the upper leaf off the bottom one, giving a convincing illusion of space. Apply a small amount of Reindeer Moss Green to enhance the lighter leaves. Blend any hard edges away with a damp brush. Using a no. 2 round brush, dab Reindeer Moss Green onto the blossoms. This is merely the background color for the flower petals. Apply Avocado to the stems with a no. 5/0 script liner. With the same brush, thin Black Green and apply it to the shaded sides of the stems. Be sure to paint the shadows of any leaves that are cast across a stem. Also there would be a slight shadow on the stems underneath the blossoms.

s t e p **4** · Load a no. 2 round brush with Titanium White, and apply the flower petals over the Reindeer Moss Green with just the brush tip. The entire bloom is made up of a cluster of small five-petal flowers. When these petals are dry, re-apply white to some of the petals on the left side of the bloom. This will lighten the white petals even more and serve as highlights. Add a few strokes of white to the bud. Using a no. 000 round brush, apply a few sepals around the base of the bloom with Avocado. Add very small dots of Antique Gold to the centers of each flower.

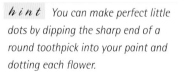

hint *You can make perfect little dots by dipping the sharp end of a round toothpick into your paint and dotting each flower.*

To vary the color of the leaves, highlight random leaves with thinned Antique Gold painted on the tips and edges. Highlight the stems by diluting Reindeer Moss Green until very fluid. Use the no. 5/0

script liner to run this color along the left sides and tops of the stems, but only adjacent to the Avocado. Where the stem is in a shadow, no highlight is applied.

Carissa carpa (Green Carpet Natal Plum)

s t e p **1** · Paint the stems with slightly thinned Avocado, using a no. 5/0 script liner brush. Paint a fine shadow of Evergreen along the right edge of the stem with the same brush. Where the leaves cast shadows onto the stem, paint Evergreen across the entire stem, then add a touch of Black Green on the part of the stem that is closest to the leaf's edge.

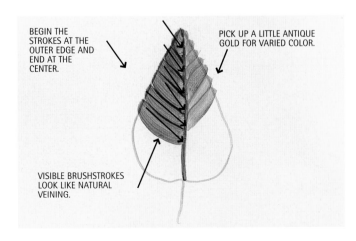

BEGIN THE STROKES AT THE OUTER EDGE AND END AT THE CENTER.

PICK UP A LITTLE ANTIQUE GOLD FOR VARIED COLOR.

VISIBLE BRUSHSTROKES LOOK LIKE NATURAL VEINING.

s t e p **2** · Paint the highlight on the stem using thinned Reindeer Moss Green. Be sure not to highlight the areas that are in the shadows. Paint the darkest leaves first. These are usually the leaves that are behind others. Use Evergreen for these darker leaves.

> *hint* DecoArt's Evergreen is more transparent compared to other greens, which is to your advantage. You want a sheer effect for your stroke marks to show up, and Evergreen will do this without having to be thinned first.

Load a ¼-inch flat shader with Evergreen. With the chisel edge of the brush, draw a line down the center of the leaf. Starting at the tip of the leaf and holding your brush almost perpendicular to the surface, drag the brush from the outside to the center line. Then, move down beside the first stroke and make another one, starting at the outer edge of the leaf and stroking in toward the center line. Don't overlap the previous strokes. Notice how the paint has streaked and the edge of the brush has left a darker line of color. It suggests veining in just one stroke.

Carissa carpa (Green Carpet Natal Plum)

s t e p **3** · Use thinned Avocado to paint the leaves using the same stroke as in step 2. For an interesting color variation, pick up a little Antique Gold on the edge of your brush after you have loaded it with Avocado. Wipe the brush back and forth to blend the gold. Then make the usual stroke on the leaf.

s t e p **4** · Paint the smallest leaves with a thinned mixture of Avocado and Reindeer Moss Green. Pick up a little Antique Gold on the brush and paint a few leaves. Use a no. 2 round brush to paint the flower petals with Titanium White. Then, float Reindeer Moss Green around the tips of the leaves that overlap the darker ones. Float Black Green onto the darkest leaves where they overlap the flower petals. Float Avocado around the bottom edges of the lightest leaves. Outline the flower petals with Reindeer Moss Green, and apply this same color to the center of the flower. Extend short lines from the center outward on the petals. Make a dot of True Ochre for each flower, and highlight that center with a smaller dot of True Ochre plus Titanium White.

Pachysandra (Japanese Spurge)

s t e p **1** · Thin Avocado to the consistency of ink. If the paint is too thick, you'll obscure your pattern lines. Using the chisel edge of a ¼-inch flat shader, paint a thin line down the center of the leaf to depict the vein. From this line, bring out ¼-inch wide strokes to the edge of the leaf, curving the stroke slightly to create a contour. Use a no. 1 round brush to paint the stems with Avocado.

s t e p **2** · Shade the darker areas and the right side of the stems with Evergreen. This includes any area where a leaf is behind another.

> *h i n t*   The leaf in the foreground will always be lighter, so use deep shading against a lighter tint to make the leaf in the back recede.

Shade deepest shadows with Black Green. Highlight the tips of the leaves with a 1:1 mixture of Avocado and Reindeer Moss Green, and occasionally tint a leaf or two with Antique Gold. Highlight the stem on left side with a mix of Avocado and Reindeer Moss Green. Be sure you allow the Avocado to separate the highlighting color and the Evergreen shadow.

s t e p **3** · Paint the flowers with Titanium White and shade near the stem with white mixed with a touch of Avocado.

The Final Touch

Seal with a light coat of polyurethane when dry. Apply the lettering after you have sealed the piece with polyurethane. Draw two light horizontal pencil lines 1 inch apart, approximately 2 inches from the bottom of the panel. Pencil in the name of the plant, then go over your lines with Glorious Gold metallic using a ¼-inch flat shader. After the gold paint is completely dry, erase any pencil marks.

Tuscan Fruit Desk

An elegant finish for just about any piece of furniture, this

olde-world look is very popular in decorating. The rich embellishments of fruit

and vines are achieved with a few surprisingly simple painting

techniques. Whether it's a den or a kitchen you're decorating, the warm

tones in this project will add a vibrant touch of Old Italy.

materials

General Supplies:
- Neutral Wall Glaze
- Dampened sea sponge
- Paper towels
- Latex gloves
- Styrofoam plate
- Pencil
- X-Acto knife
- Americana Brush 'n' Blend (Extender)

Brushes:
- no. 3 mop brush or 2" hake brush
- no. 5/0 script liner
- ½" dagger striper
- ½" rake
- ¼" and ½" flat shader
- nos. 0 and 2 round

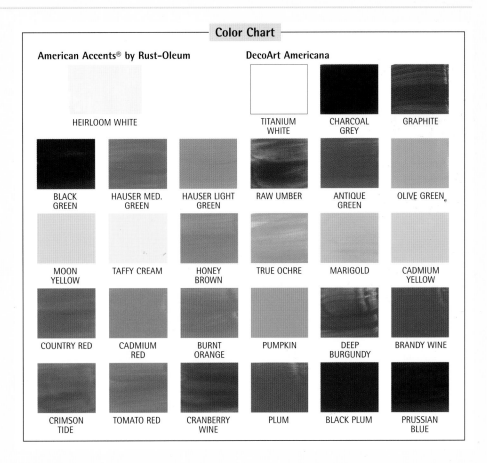

Color Chart

American Accents® by Rust-Oleum

DecoArt Americana

HEIRLOOM WHITE	TITANIUM WHITE · CHARCOAL GREY	GRAPHITE
BLACK GREEN · HAUSER MED. GREEN · HAUSER LIGHT GREEN	RAW UMBER · ANTIQUE GREEN	OLIVE GREEN
MOON YELLOW · TAFFY CREAM · HONEY BROWN	TRUE OCHRE · MARIGOLD	CADMIUM YELLOW
COUNTRY RED · CADMIUM RED · BURNT ORANGE	PUMPKIN · DEEP BURGUNDY	BRANDY WINE
CRIMSON TIDE · TOMATO RED · CRANBERRY WINE	PLUM · BLACK PLUM	PRUSSIAN BLUE

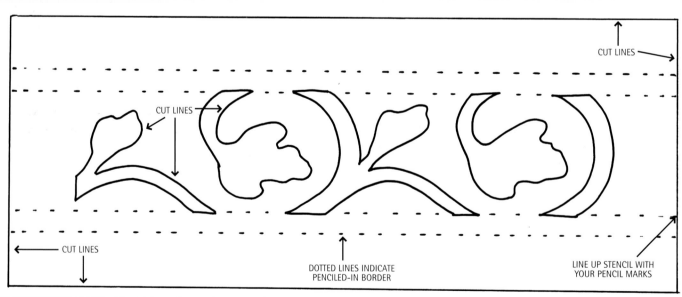

CUT LINES

CUT LINES

CUT LINES

DOTTED LINES INDICATE
PENCILED-IN BORDER

LINE UP STENCIL WITH
YOUR PENCIL MARKS

THESE PATTERNS MAY BE HAND-TRACED OR PHOTOCOPIED FOR PERSONAL USE ONLY.
ENLARGE AT 115% TO BRING THEM UP TO FULL SIZE.

Create a Subtle Stucco Finish

s t e p **1** · Prepare and prime the surface as instructed on page 15. Apply a base coat of Heirloom White. Use two coats if necessary. Let this dry overnight. In a shallow container, mix thoroughly 2 parts Neutral Wall Glaze to 1 part Honey Brown. (About one cup of this mixture will cover a large piece of furniture.)

s t e p **2** · Take a dry mop brush in the hand you normally paint with, and with the other hand, dip one side of a dampened sea sponge into the Honey Brown glaze mix. For a detailed explanation of this technique, see steps 2 and 3 on page 21.)

s t e p **3** · With a light touch, immediately begin diffusing the glaze mix with the mop brush, making Xs and figure eights in the glaze. Leave no pattern in the glaze. Let this layer of glaze dry approximately two hours. Save the leftover glaze mix.

s t e p **4** · Mix 2 parts Neutral Wall Glaze with 1 part Heirloom White, and repeat the entire process on top of the first glaze mixture to soften the effect.

Create a Subtle Stucco Finish

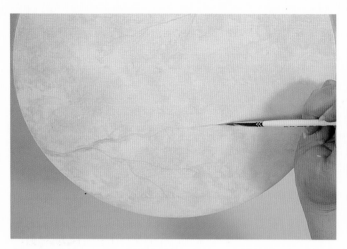

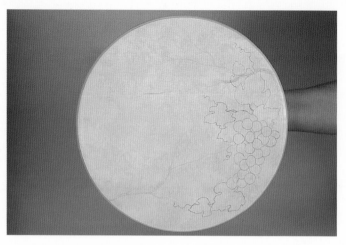

step **5** · Add a few random "cracks" and imperfections in the subtle stucco finish by loading your ½-inch dagger striper with the Honey Brown glaze mixture and dragging it across the surface, twisting the brush as you drag.

step **6** · Let this dry overnight before applying any decorative painting. Save any unused glaze mixture if you plan to add the decorative frieze border.

Create Antique Mossing

step **1** · Mix 2 parts Avocado (DecoArt Americana) with 1 part Raw Umber, then add 3 parts Neutral Wall Glaze and mix well.

step **2** · Apply mossing sparingly and randomly with a small sponge to seams and inside corners and around knobs. (Use a small brush to get in corners and crevices.)

step **3** · Then immediately diffuse the paint with the dry mop brush, using the small figure eights and Xs mentioned earlier. All edges of the mossing should blend into transparency.

Add a Decorative Frieze Border

Applying some trim to your project adds interest to the "Tuscan" look and helps break up any large surfaces or enhance an existing edge or molding. Add this feature after the glaze coat is dry, but before any fruit or vines are painted.

With a pencil, lightly mark off ¼-inch borders that are 1½-inches apart. Trace the pattern of the frieze onto card stock or heavy paper and cut it out with an X-Acto knife. Line up your stencil within the border lines and lightly pencil in the design. Place the stencil next to the design you just penciled in and continue transferring the motif between the borders. For photographic purposes, I have made fairly heavy lines here, but you need to use the lightest pencil marks possible. Erase the marks where the stems on the motif meet the ¼-inch borders.

s t e p **1** · Mix 2 parts Neutral Wall Glaze with 1 part Heirloom White for a translucent mixture and paint the motif and border using a ¼-inch flat shader, letting the color underneath show through.

s t e p **2** · Mix 1 part Honey Brown with 1 part Neutral Wall Glaze. Dab this mixture along the bottom edges of the frieze where a shadow would be cast.

s t e p **3** · The carved, sculptured look of this frieze is achieved by the illusions of highlight and shadow. For the highlight, lightly dab Heirloom White along the top edges of the motif, covering the pencil line. Don't make the line perfect, as that would suggest a smooth surface and the stucco look needs to appear rough. A small scruffy brush is ideal for this.

To see how to paint the grape leaves refer to page 22.

Paint the Fruit

Painted fruit looks classy on just about anything, and for that reason I have broken up the cluster of fruit from this project into individual step-by-step studies. I don't recommend reducing or enlarging the pattern as fruit looks best if it's painted life-size. So if your painting surface calls for something a bit smaller than the pattern, create your own cluster of fruit by taking only two or three components from the pattern and painting them.

APPLES

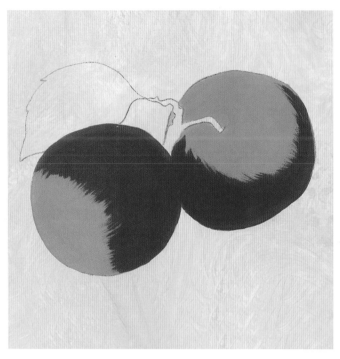 

s t e p 1 · Using a ½-inch shader, basecoat the apples with True Ochre and let dry. Paint portions of each apple with Tomato Red, as shown, tapering off the ends of your strokes to produce an irregular, dry-brush effect. Proceed immediately to the next step before the Tomato Red dries.

s t e p 2 · Mix a small amount of Tomato Red with True Ochre to make a yellow-orange mix. Dip a damp rake brush into extender, and then into the yellow-orange color. Before the Tomato Red has dried, apply the yellow-orange mixture in short strokes to the ragged edge of the Tomato Red until the two sections are smoothly blended. Let this dry.

Mix 1 part Cranberry Wine with 1 part extender, then dilute with water until runny. Using a ½-inch rake brush, make light strokes over the red areas, from the upper stem to the bottom of the apple. Arch your strokes to follow the contour of the apple.

s t e p **3** · Paint the stem with Graphite. Thin Hauser Light Green to the consistency of ink and paint a thin line from the stem to the tip of the leaf with the chisel edge of a shader. With the flat side of the brush paint arched strokes of green across and down the entire length of the leaf, stopping at the center vein. The paint should be transparent so your strokes are visible.

On the right side of the left apple, shade the Tomato Red area with Cranberry Wine. Do the same on the right apple where a shadow is cast. Using the rake brush, add a patch of Olive Green to the apple's skin, starting at the stem and stroking outward. Be sure to follow the contour of the apple. With the green left on the brush, dab a small amount around the base of the stem and on the bottom of the left apple. Blend into the yellow mixture with a damp, clean brush. Shade the green area around the top stem with Hauser Medium Green.

s t e p **4** · Side-load a ½-inch flat shader with Black Green and float it around the outer edges of the leaf and against the apple. Float Black Plum along the inside of the right apple to create the deepest shading. Mix Titanium White with Graphite to get a medium gray. Paint along the left side of the stem. Dab a few strokes of Titanium White on top of this gray to highlight. Use a small round brush to shade the right side of the stem with Charcoal Grey. Also apply Charcoal Grey to the very base of the stem. With the paint left on the brush, add Hauser Medium Green to get a gray-green and detail the blossom end on the left apple.

Thin a small amount of Cadmium Yellow until watery. Using the rake brush, apply contouring to the highlighted side of the left apple. Do not apply yellow strokes over the dark areas. Dilute a small amount of Titanium White until it's the consistency of ink, and highlight the apples using short strokes with the rake brush.

Paint the Fruit

CHERRIES

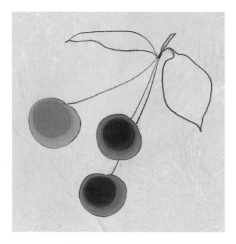

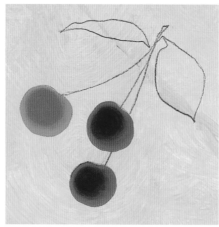

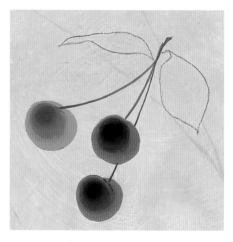

s t e p 1 · For interesting cherries, paint them in different stages of ripeness. For the unripe cherry, using a ¼-inch flat shader, basecoat with Pumpkin using Titanium White as an undercoat. Basecoat the ripe cherries with Cadmium Red. Paint a circle of Cadmium Red, off-center, on the unripe cherry. Do the same for the ripe cherries using Deep Burgundy.

s t e p 2 · Mix a 2:1 ratio of Pumpkin and Cadmium Red to get an "in between" color. Apply to the outside of the circle on the unripe cherry and blend the two colors together. Do the same for the ripe cherries with Cadmium Red and Deep Burgundy.

s t e p 3 · Paint a smaller circle using a ¼-inch flat shader loaded with Country Red inside the circle of Cadmium Red on the unripe cherry. Blend this color into the previous one by the same method shown in step 2, but use a 2:1 mix of Cadmium Red and Country Red. The ripe cherries are painted the same way, but using Black Plum as the darkest color and blending with a mixture of Deep Burgundy and Black Plum. Paint a fine line with a 5/0 script liner loaded with Deep Burgundy where the stem attaches. Don't paint dimples on all the cherries. Paint the stems Hauser Medium Green using a no. 5/0 script liner.

s t e p 4 · Paint a dot or two of Titanium White in the darkest part of each cherry, off-center just a bit. Using a no. 1 round brush, paint a thin line of Cadmium Yellow on the right side of the unripe cherry. Do the same on the darker cherries using Pumpkin.

Follow the apple leaf instructions on page 51 to paint the cherry leaves.

PEARS

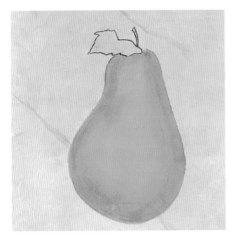

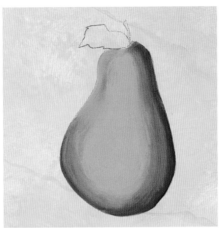

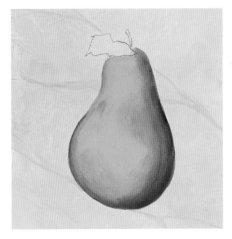

s t e p **1** · Basecoat the pear with two coats of Marigold and let dry. Float full-strength True Ochre roughly around the outer edge of the pear using a ½ -inch shader. Ordinarily, I take great care when floating colors, but this is a pear, and although it has a smooth surface, its flesh is soft and marred with small dents and bruises.

s t e p **2** · Dilute Raw Umber to the consistency of ink. Sideload a ½ -inch shader and float along the right side, tapering the float at the pear's bottom center. Make a thin wash of Brandy Wine. When the Raw Umber is dry, apply the wash to the right side of the pear, following the contour with a ½ -inch shader. Rinse the brush and blot it on a paper towel. Run the brush over the float's inside edge to diffuse any hard lines. Float thinned Antique Green along the bottom left edge.

s t e p **3** · Dip the brush back into the Antique Green. Then wipe off all you can onto a paper towel. Dry brush a few patches of Antique Green onto the pear, but keep it light and don't apply any in the center.

Dilute Burnt Orange as thin as you did the Antique Green. Float a hint of color along the upper left side of the pear. Load the tip of the brush again with the thinned Burnt Orange and dry brush a few patches. When applying these two dry-brushed colors, apply them around the contour of the pear, at the neck and bottom of the fruit. Since these colors are darker than the base coat of Marigold, they recede and give the illusion of dimension and shape.

s t e p **4** · With all the shading applied, there should still be areas in the center of the pear, bottom and neck, where the Marigold is seen. For the pear to take on a realistic shape, this color must show through. If you have applied too much shading and the Marigold is obscured, now is the time to correct it. Re-apply Marigold to the bottom and neck if needed, blending the edges away with a clean, damp brush.

With a ½ -inch rake brush, apply Cadmium Yellow to the center left of the lower part of the pear in a circular patch, no bigger than a penny. This highlight of Cadmium Yellow must not touch any of the

Antique Green or Burnt Orange shading; it should be surrounded by Marigold on all sides. When the Cadmium Yellow is dry, add the final highlight, a few dabs of diluted Titanium White with a no. 2 round brush.

> *hint* Pears are not naturally glossy fruit, so it is important to dilute the Titanium White before applying it. Otherwise, it might suggest a sharp reflection of light.

The stem and bud are painted with Raw Umber, using just the tip of a no. 2 round brush. Follow the apple leaf instructions to add the pear leaf.

BLACKBERRIES

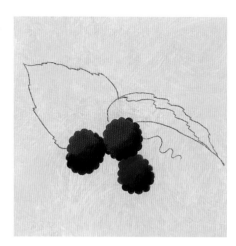

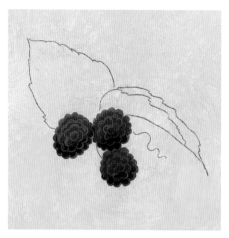

s t e p 1 · Basecoat the berries with Black Plum and let dry. On the upper half of two berries, apply Plum. On the third berry, apply Crimson Tide.

s t e p 2 · Mix Titanium White into Plum enough to slightly lighten it, and dilute it to the consistency of ink. With a no. 5/0 liner brush, outline the outer scalloped edge. Move inside and paint another scalloped row very close to the first, but stagger it slightly. Continue until you get to the center of the berry, where you'll paint one or two round circles. On the upper part of the berry use the same color and paint tiny comma strokes on each seed for a highlight.

s t e p 3 · Add more Titanium White to the light Plum mix and Crimson Tide and highlight the outer edges of the upper-left seeds, using a no. 5/0 liner brush. Dampen the leaves with clear water using a ¼ -inch shader. Load the brush with Hauser Medium Green and run the chisel edge lightly down the center of the leaf. Put the chisel edge against the leaf's outline at the tip and pull the brush down to the center vein you just painted and halfway down the leaf. With the dirty brush, pick up a bit of Black Green and continue making strokes. Rinse the brush and load it with Antique Green, and repeat the process. If the center vein looks irregular now, you can run the chisel edge of the brush along it to correct the line. If the water on the curled leaf has dried by this time, rewet it and paint the inside Antique Green and the underside Black Green. When both leaves are thoroughly dry, re-wet the left leaf with clear water. Pick up a small amount of Plum on a no. 2 round brush and apply to the tip of the leaf. Rinse the brush and pull the color out into the leaf until it disappears, leaving a tiny concentration of color at the very edge of the leaf. Apply a stronger coat of Black Green to the base of both leaves where they meet the berries. Paint the tendril and stem Antique Green and add shading with Black Green.

s t e p 4 · If you have allowed your strokes to create the veins, it should be enough. But if you prefer, drag out veins from the center line using Hauser Medium Green with a no. 5/0 liner.

Add highlights to the berries using Titanium White and a no. 0 round brush. Make the highlights small comma strokes on all the seeds. On the side of the berries that reflects the light, apply a tiny half-moon line of white around the outer edges of a few seeds.

Add the Ribbon

The ribbon is used in this project for continuity and helps connect the artwork on this unusually large desktop. Here the color of the ribbon is kept very close to the background, so its appearance is subtle.

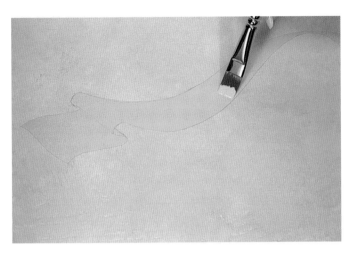

s t e p **1** · Basecoat the ribbon Moon Yellow and let dry.

s t e p **2** · With a ¼-inch flat shader, apply Taffy Cream for highlights, blending it smoothly into the Moon Yellow.

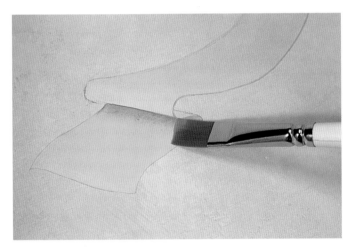

s t e p **3** · Shade the ribbon with a float of Honey Brown on a ½-inch shader.

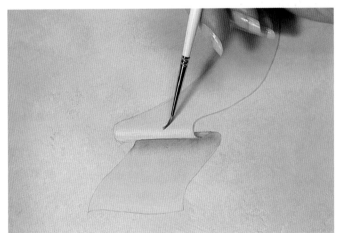

s t e p **4** · Highlight the edges of the ribbon with wisps of Titanium White using a no. 1 script liner. Blend them into the Moon Yellow.

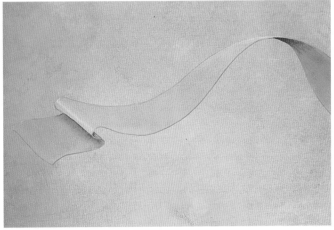

Detail of Ribbon

The Final Touches

SHADOWS

A shadow is not necessary in your design, but it will seemingly lift the object right off the surface and become the final touch in your strive for realism.

Mix 2 parts Raw Umber to 1 part Prussian Blue and 1 part Graphite. Add 7 parts water to 1 part of this mixture. The result should be a thin, transparent wash with just a hint of color to it. Apply with a ¼-inch shader to the background on the side of the object opposite the light source. For example, if the light is coming from above, then your shadows are cast below the object.

Detail of the decorative frieze border

Fruit detail

Detail of twisting ivy on leg

Ribbon details

Northwoods Blanket Chest

Blanket chests date back several centuries. They were designed for storing

quilts and blankets. Today, they are still great for storage, and can easily double

as a coffee or end table. Their plain, basic lines also make them ideal painting

surfaces, and their versatility allows them to fit into any decorating theme. So

when I wanted to paint an Adirondack theme on something, I chose this blan-

ket chest because it would feel at home in any cozy den or mountain retreat.

materials

General Supplies:
- Carver-Tripp® Safe and Simple ™ Wood Stain (Special Walnut)
- Straight edge
- Pencil
- Paper towels
- Latex gloves
- Satin waterbased polyurethane
- Painter's tape (low tack)

Brushes:
- 1- and 2-inch foam brushes
- no. 5/0 script liner
- nos. 0 and 1 round
- $1/4$" ,$1/2$", and 1" flat shader
- $1/4$" cat's tongue
- $1/2$" rake
- no. 0 round
- $1/2$" dagger striper
- $1/4$" mop brush
- $1/4$" filbert
- no. 2 fan brush
- scruffy brush or deerfoot stippler

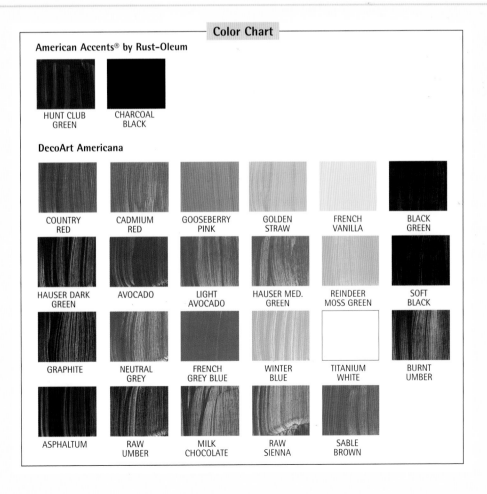

Color Chart

American Accents® by Rust-Oleum

HUNT CLUB GREEN · CHARCOAL BLACK

DecoArt Americana

COUNTRY RED · CADMIUM RED · GOOSEBERRY PINK · GOLDEN STRAW · FRENCH VANILLA · BLACK GREEN

HAUSER DARK GREEN · AVOCADO · LIGHT AVOCADO · HAUSER MED. GREEN · REINDEER MOSS GREEN · SOFT BLACK

GRAPHITE · NEUTRAL GREY · FRENCH GREY BLUE · WINTER BLUE · TITANIUM WHITE · BURNT UMBER

ASPHALTUM · RAW UMBER · MILK CHOCOLATE · RAW SIENNA · SABLE BROWN

Landscape pattern

THIS PATTERN MAY BE HAND-TRACED OR
PHOTOCOPIED FOR PERSONAL USE ONLY.
ENLARGE AT 122% TO BRING IT UP TO
FULL SIZE.

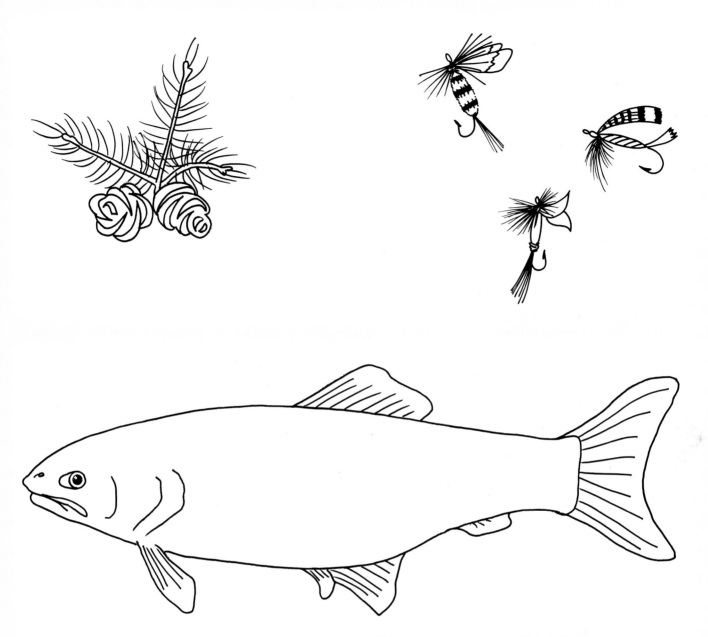

THESE PATTERNS MAY BE HAND-TRACED OR PHOTOCOPIED FOR PERSONAL USE ONLY.
ENLARGE AT 141% TO BRING THEM UP TO FULL SIZE.

Prepare the Surface

Prepare surface as instructed on page 15. Stain the chest inside and any areas outside that you want wood-stained. Follow the manufacturer's instructions on the can. Let this dry completely. Since staining raises the grain of the wood, sand the chest lightly after it has dried and then remove the dust.

With a straightedge and pencil, mark off the framed areas that will be the landscape and trout paintings. Enlarge and transfer the patterns to your surface. Basecoat the chest with Hunt Club Green and the lid with Charcoal Black, except the areas you marked off.

Paint the Northwoods Landscape

I wanted a more masculine effect on this chest, so I omitted the sky on mine. If you opt to include a sky in your project, I've included the instructions.

s t e p **1** · Paint the upper sky area Winter Blue with a 1-inch flat shader. Use long, horizontal sweeps with the brush. Add a bit of Titanium White to Winter Blue and paint the area below the area you just painted. Blend the two colors together, and continue painting the sky with lighter tints of blue until you reach the horizon. Paint the same blue tints in the stream, using horizontal strokes parallel to the horizon. Make the water that is furthest away lighter than the water in the foreground.

s t e p **2** · Load the outer edges of a ¼-inch filbert with Titanium White and tap in clouds just above the horizon. Smooth the undersides of the clouds into transparency with a damp brush.

Basecoat the mountains with French Grey Blue. Add Graphite to the French Grey Blue to make a darker blue and apply on the left side of the mountains for shadow.

HOW TO PAINT DISTANT FOLIAGE

Create distant foliage by dabbing Reindeer Moss Green along the furthest line of foliage. Use the rounded edge of a ½-inch scruffy brush or deerfoot stippler to suggest the tops of distant trees.

The next line of foliage will be darker and appear more detailed, so your brushstroke will differ. Wet the mop brush and load with Light Avocado. Dab the excess on a paper towel. Hold the brush perpendicular to the surface just below the first line of foliage. Press the brush down gently so the bristles bend away from you. Giving a short flick of the brush, pull it away from the surface. Make this type of stroke along the entire foliage line. Add Black Green to the Light Avocado for a darker shade and apply it as another row of foliage. Apply Black Green at the base of this last foliage.

Paint the Northwoods Landscape

s t e p **3** · Apply Winter Blue to the right sides of the mountaintops with the chisel edge of a ¼ -inch flat shader. Paint the furthest grass Light Avocado, bringing the grass line up to the bottom edge of the Black Green in the foliage. Paint around the trees and cabin, using small upward strokes with a ¼ -inch flat shader. As you work downward, darken the grass by switching to Avocado. Also switch to a ½ -inch flat shader for larger areas, but continue the upward stroke to suggest the directional growth of the grass. Add Black Green to the Avocado for a darker color. As you near the bottom of the painting, the grass should not only appear darker than what's in the distance, but the blades of grass will appear longer also, so make your strokes longer.

Apply Black Green shadows to the left sides of individual trees, and to the left of the cabin and boat. Also add shadow at the base of the thicket on the right and along the waterline on the right bank of the stream.

s t e p **4** · With the chisel edge of a shader, add Titanium White to the right side of the mountains. Apply it on top of the Winter Blue, but do not fully obscure the original color. Basecoat the cabin Milk Chocolate, the roof Sable Brown, and the chimney a mixture of Neutral Grey and Titanium White. Add a bit more Titanium White and highlight the chimney on the right side. Basecoat the boat with Country Red. Add a touch of Soft Black to the Country Red and paint the inside of the boat with this darker color. Also use this color to shade the bow of the boat.

How to Paint the Trees

* Block in the trees and thicket with Black Green. Apply the branches on the evergreens with the corner of the fan brush. Apply the trees' first highlights with Light Avocado by stippling on the right side of the tree with a scruffy brush. The final tree highlight is done with the scruffy brush and Reindeer Moss Green. Apply the final highlight over the Light Avocado, but do not completely cover it up.

s t e p **5** · Define the foliage by stippling branches with Light Avocado. Stippling is achieved by pouncing color onto the surface with a dry scruffy brush and full-strength paint. Dip the tip of the brush into the paint and blot it on a paper towel. Stipple this color on the right-side branches of the trees and shrubs. Suggest shrubbery on the right bank by stippling in a few clumps with Light Avocado.

Suggest a reflection in the water by loading a rake brush with thinned Avocado. Blot lightly onto a paper towel. Make light strokes from the edge of the bank straight down.

Make the logs across the side and front of the cabin using a no. 1 round loaded with diluted Sable Brown, and a thin path in front of the porch. Add a touch of Titanium White to the Sable Brown and highlight areas of the roof using a ¼ -inch flat shader.

Load Neutral Grey on a no. 0 round brush and dab rocks on the chimney. Make the rocks look randomly stacked, yet close together. Add a touch of Titanium White to make the rocks on the right side of the chimney. Scatter a few rocks in the stream with this light gray color. Apply a shadow to each rock with Neutral Grey.

s t e p **6** · Stipple Reindeer Moss Green sparingly onto the lighter branches of the thicket and shrubbery with the scruffy brush.

Apply thinned Titanium White with a no. 5/0 liner brush along the edge of the waterline on the right bank and around the edges of the rocks. Dilute Titanium White a bit more and create fine ribbons of reflection on top of the water's surface. Use this same solution and the no. 1 round brush to paint a soft cloud of smoke coming from the chimney and to highlight the right sides of the rocks.

Highlight the rim of the boat and suggest a couple of bench seats with Cadmium Red using the no. 0 round.

Using the no. 0 round, add shadows to the cabin with Raw Umber between the logs, under the eaves and porch roof. Shade the cabin on the left side of the chimney and the left sides of the porch posts. Add a porch rail in Raw Umber and highlight with Sable Brown mixed with a touch of Titanium White. Apply a few streaks of this highlight to the path with the ¼ -inch flat shader. Add a door to the cabin using the no. 0 round loaded with Raw Umber deepened with a touch of Soft Black.

Create wisps of grass along the bank and around the boat and cabin with Avocado and the fan brush. Use a no. 5/0 liner brush loaded with Light Avocado to stroke out tall grass in the left foreground and on the right at the edge of the water. Since this grass is closer than any other it will be the longest in the painting. Make Xs of Titanium White with the no. 5/0 liner to depict blooms among the grass on the left, and use Raw Umber to paint cattails along the water bank on the right. Paint a few tiny birds in the sky by making a squat V with a fine-pointed no. 5/0 liner and Raw Umber. When the landscape is dry, add a coat of waterbased satin polyurethane using a 2-inch foam brush.

Paint the Rainbow Trout

s t e p **1** · Basecoat the fish with Light Avocado and let dry. Mix a 1:1 blend of Titanium White and Light Avocado, and paint the lower part of the fish and highlight the fins and tail. Define the gills, mouth and eye.

Use a ½ -inch flat shader to run a streak of watery Gooseberry Pink down the side of the fish's body—from the eye to the base of the tail. Blend any hard lines with a damp brush.

s t e p **2** · Add more Titanium White to the light green mixture to create an even lighter green. Paint the eyeball using a no. 0 round. Using a 1-inch flat shader, float Hauser Dark Green along the top edge of the fish. Using this same color and brush, apply to the base of the tail, feathering out toward the end of the tail. Use a no. 5/0 liner brush to define the gills, eye, mouth, and ridges on the fins and tail.

s t e p **3** · Paint the pupil Soft Black. Thin Titanium White until transparent. Load a dagger striper with the thinned Titanium White and blot on a paper towel. You don't want so much paint to flow from the brush that it will puddle on the surface. Place the chisel point of the brush down first, then where the line needs to get wider, turn the brush so most of the bristles are laying down paint. Return the brush to its chisel point to taper the stroke into a thin line again. Run the same kind of highlight down the side of the fish's belly.

Use a no. 1 round loaded with the thinned Titanium White to highlight the ends of the fins and tail. Use the same brush but a stronger value of Titanium White to highlight the gills, mouth, nostril and eye.

Speckle areas using Hauser Dark Green dabbed on with a no. 1 round brush. Refer to the photo for placement of the spots. Mix a bit of Titanium White

with Hauser Dark Green to lighten the speckles on top of the highlight area. In the darkest areas, such as the base of the tail and the top edge of the trout's back, use Black Green for the spots. Add tiny speckles of Titanium White inside the highlighted area of the fish's back. Add a dot of Titanium White to the fish's eye.

The Final Touches

ADD THE PINE SPRIGS

s t e p **1** · Paint the stems Milk Chocolate with a no. 1 round brush. Basecoat the cones with Burnt Umber and a ¼ -inch flat shader.

s t e p **2** · Shade one side of stems with Burnt Umber and a no. 5/0 liner brush. With a no. 1 round brush and arched strokes of Milk Chocolate, suggest pinecone scales.

s t e p **3** · Generously load a no. 5/0 liner with thinned Hauser Dark Green and paint needles using short, quick, curving strokes, starting at the stem and stroking outward. Deepen the shading in the pinecone with Asphaltum.

s t e p **4** · Add lighter needles using Hauser Medium Green. Highlight the tips of the pinecone scales with Raw Sienna, with a touch of French Vanilla blended into the Raw Sienna at the very edge for enhanced highlight. Add a touch of Soft Black to Asphaltum and deepen the darkest crevices in the pinecones.

The Final Touches

● ADD THE TROUT FLIES

A few trout flies can be placed about to help define that masculine
theme in a whimsical way. Here are three common ones, but you
can add as many as you want by varying the color and style of the fly.
Just remember to stick to natural hues (yellows, greens, browns)
when painting flies and lures.

*s t e p **1**·* Block in the base colors. Pat-blend the gray in the
wings into the black.

*s t e p **2**·* Add contouring with either darker or lighter values.

*s t e p **3**·* Add the highlights and detail.

Detail of trout flies.

ADD THE BUFFALO PLAID

To mimic a buffalo plaid design as I did on the drawer, basecoat the drawer with Country Red first.

s t e p **1** · Place low tack tape vertically on your surface. Apply your first layer of thinned Charcoal Black stripes where the tape isn't using a 1-inch foam brush. Let this dry about twenty-four hours.

s t e p **2** · After the first layer has dried, remove the vertical tape. Apply horizontal stripes of low tack tape on your surface. Apply Charcoal Black paint as you did in step 1.

s t e p **3** · Carefully remove the tape. There is less resistance on both the tape and the painted surface if the tape is pulled up at a 90 ° angle. Don't rip the tape off, yet don't pull too slowly either. I find the best time to remove tape is when the paint has just dried and is still tacky.

Detail of Buffalo Plaid

Make your stripes streaky so the only place there is solid black is where the stripes intersect as on real buffalo plaid. Here I was unhappy to see my paint had seeped under the tape (burnish those edges!) but realized the feathered paint had softened the stripes, much like real wool.

Garden Shed Cabinet

I really like the look of brick, yet when this garden-theme cabinet needed a background, I hesitated, fearing the brick might be too strong. But the light and airy lattice on top balances the look. This piece is great to brighten up a kitchen or sunroom, and will look terrific on any number of cabinets or hutches. Even if your surface is just a set of shelves, the lattice and ivy techniques work well to achieve a garden look. Knowing that the doors are going to be the focal point of this piece, I use non-competing neutral colors on the rest of the cabinet. Heavy, overpowering colors on this type of project wouldn't work. In my opinion, a garden theme on any surface requires light, natural, sunny colors.

materials

General Supplies:
- 1" painter's tape (low tack)
- X-Acto knife
- White and black transfer paper
- Pencil
- Small sea sponge
- Paper towels
- Latex gloves
- Waterbased Satin Polyurethane

Brushes:
- nos. 1 and 2 round brush
- 1/4", 1/2" and 1" flat shaders
- no. 2 and 5/0 script liner
- 1/2" deerfoot stippler

Prepare the Surface

Prepare the surface as instructed on page 15. Basecoat the lattice work area with Heirloom White. Basecoat the remaining surface with Ivory Silk. Paint the baseboard trim with Moss Green and the door frames with Taupe.

American Accents® by Rust-Oleum

MOSS GREEN

IVORY SILK

TAUPE

HEIRLOOM WHITE

DecoArt Americana

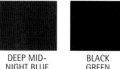
DEEP MID-NIGHT BLUE

BLACK GREEN

AVOCADO

PLANTATION PINE

EVERGREEN

HAUSER DARK GREEN

LIGHT AVOCADO

ANTIQUE GREEN

HAUSER LIGHT GREEN

DRIED BASIL GREEN

REINDEER MOSS GREEN

SOFT BLACK

GRAPHITE

NEUTRAL GREY

SLATE GREY

GREY SKY

ASPHALTUM

ANTIQUE MAROON

BURNT SIENNA

OXBLOOD

DELANES DEEP SHADOW

TERRA COTTA

SHADING FLESH

CADMIUM RED

CHERRY RED

BERRY RED

NAPA RED

BRANDY WINE

DEEP BURGUNDY

ROOKWOOD RED

BLACK PLUM

PUMPKIN

OLDE GOLD

HONEY BROWN

CAMEL

KHAKI TAN

FRENCH VANILLA

BUTTERMILK

TITANIUM WHITE

LILAC

GLORIOUS GOLD

Brick Pattern

THIS PATTERN MAY
BE HAND-TRACED
OR PHOTOCOPIED
FOR PERSONAL USE
ONLY. ENLARGE AT
200%, THEN AT 112%
TO BRING IT UP TO
FULL SIZE.

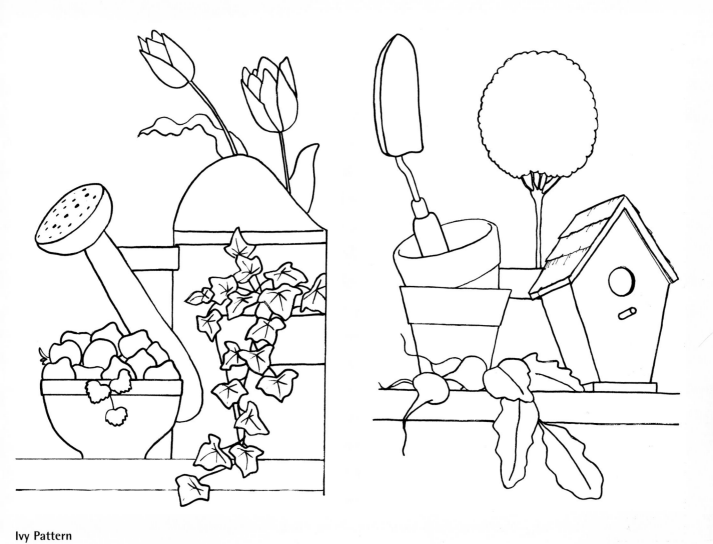

Ivy Pattern

Paint the Lattice Work

s t e p **1** · Basecoat the surface with Heirloom White latex paint and let dry twenty-four hours before beginning the lattice work. Apply painter's tape at a 45 ° angle. Allow the tape edges to extend over the edge of your surface. To space your tape evenly, lay the tape down side by side, then remove every other strip.

s t e p **2** · Use the same method to apply tape across the first layer at the opposite angle making Xs. Burnish the tape edges.

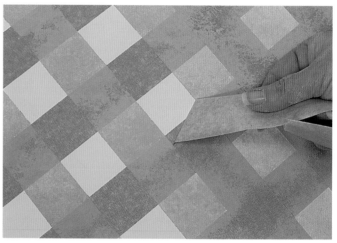

s t e p **3** · Tint Heirloom White with Deep Midnight Blue, drop-by-drop until you arrive at a light blue color. Dampen a small sea sponge and wring it out. Sponge on the color in all the square openings. Sponging the paint on is less likely to lift the edges of the tape so the paint won't seep under.

s t e p **4** · Gently remove the tape when the paint is dry to reveal the lattice work pattern.

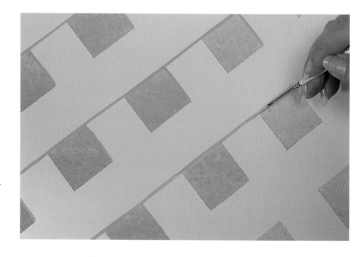

s t e p **5** · Apply Grey Sky with a no. 2 liner brush on the bottom edge of each lattice strip for shadowing. Remember, all the strips going one way will be in front, and the other crisscrossing strips are in the back.

Add the Ivy

s t e p **1** · Draw a vine that winds in and out of the lattice slats and trails down over the doors. Use the pattern to transfer the ivy leaves. Paint the vine and stems Avocado using a no. 2 liner. Load your ½-inch flat shader with Avocado. Dip one corner into Black Green, and the other in Titanium White. Wipe back and forth on your palette to blend the colors. Paint the leaves with teardrop shaped strokes, flipping the brush for color variety.

s t e p **2** · Rinse your brush and reload it, only this time load it with the darker Avocado mix and Black Green and Titanium White on the chisel end. This variation will make a slightly different colored leaf, adding interest and dimension to the vine.

s t e p **3** · Make a third larger stroke in the middle of the two others, and end the stroke at the base of the leaf.

s t e p **4** · Mix Titanium White and Avocado to get a very pale green and apply fine veins to each leaf with a 5/0 script liner.

Detail of the Ivy

Paint the Brick Background

Transfer the brick pattern on page 74 to heavy stock paper. Carefully cut out the brick shapes with an X-Acto knife. Hold the stencil against your background and trace the bricks onto the door with a pencil. Be sure to allow a ½-inch mortar space between the bricks when you move the stencil around. Even though there will be objects in front of much of this brick, do the entire background anyway.

Put generous amounts of Brandy Wine, Oxblood, DeLane's Deep Shadow and Shading Flesh and a small amount of Antique Green on your palette. Put several layers of paper towel beside your palette.

s t e p **1** · Paint mortar lines with two coats of Khaki Tan using a ½-inch flat shader.

s t e p **2** · Dampen a medium-sized sea sponge. Replace brick stencil and pick up a generous amount of Brandy Wine with the sponge. Blot off excess on a paper towel. Sponge Brandy Wine over all the bricks. Take care to keep your stencil in place to protect the mortar color.

s t e p 3 · Sponge Oxblood over the Brandy Wine in the same manner. It doesn't matter whether the first color is dry or not, but be sure to rinse the sponge before changing colors. Turn the sponge to keep from making patterned marks, and sponge lightly enough to let the first color show through. Apply DeLane's Deep Shadow in the same manner, taking care to keep the sponging light and allowing the previous colors to show through the new layer. Finally, apply Shading Flesh sparingly to highlight the brick.

Dilute Antique Green to a wash and apply it with a ¼-inch mop to areas of brick and mortar to suggest the presence of moss. A little green goes a long way, so keep this wash very light and transparent.

s t e p 4 · Assume your light source is coming from the upper left. Highlight the top and left edges of each brick with a thin line of Shading Flesh using a small round or liner brush. Mix equal amounts of Prussian Blue and Charcoal Grey to make a transparent wash, then add a touch of Raw Umber. Apply this mixture to the mortar (next to the right edge and bottom edges of the bricks) with a small round or liner brush to create a shadow and add depth.

For realistic detail, create cracks in a few bricks by applying Asphaltum with a no. 5/0 liner. Starting at the edge of the brick, drag the brush at an angle and twist the handle as you go, creating a jagged line and a rough "Y" shape. On the edges of the crack where the light would hit, make a very thin line of Shading Flesh.

Paint the Tulip & Strawberry Still Life

After your background is completely dry, transfer the still life patterns onto your surface using white transfer paper. Transfer only the main shapes, omitting the individual strawberries, the strawberry leaves and ivy.

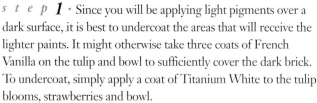

s t e p **1** · Since you will be applying light pigments over a dark surface, it is best to undercoat the areas that will receive the lighter paints. It might otherwise take three coats of French Vanilla on the tulip and bowl to sufficiently cover the dark brick. To undercoat, simply apply a coat of Titanium White to the tulip blooms, strawberries and bowl.

After the undercoat is dry, basecoat in the tulips and bowl with French Vanilla, the tulip leaves with Avocado, the watering can with Slate Grey, the flowerpot with Terra Cotta, the strawberries with Berry Red, and the table with Rookwood Red.

s t e p **2** · In this project, the light is coming from the upper left, so the objects have more shading on the right sides. Shade the tulips and bowl by floating Camel along the edges as shown with a ¼ -inch flat shader. Shade the tulip leaves with Evergreen. Run the same color down the right of the stem with a no. 2 script liner.

Shade the watering can with a mixture of 1 part Deep Midnight Blue, 1 part Graphite, and 1 part Titanium White. I found dry-brushing this shade on was more effective in giving the can a worn look. But apply it strongest where the deep shadows would fall—to the right of the bowl and on the stem just below the spout.

With a 1-inch flat shader, float Burnt Sienna along the outer edges of the flowerpot. Then, with the chisel edge, draw a line to depict the bottom edge of the rim.

Carefully reposition your pattern, slip black transfer paper underneath, and transfer the individual strawberries. Using a ¼ -inch flat shader, outline and shade the strawberries with Napa Red. Shade beneath the overhang of the table by floating Black Plum with a ½ -inch flat shader. For a perfectly straight line, apply Scotch Brand Magic Tape along this line, press down edges firmly, and paint against the edge of the tape. Gently remove tape when paint is dry.

s t e p **3** · Using a ½ -inch flat shader, highlight on the upper left of the tulips and bowl with Buttermilk. Dry brush Pumpkin over the Terra Cotta on the flowerpot with a horizontal stroke from a ½ -inch flat shader. With a ¼ -inch flat shader, paint the left side of the strawberries with Cadmium Red. With the same brush, highlight the edge of the leaves with Dried Basil Green. Dry brush Grey Sky highlights onto the watering can with the ½ -inch shader, and run a line of Cherry Red along the upper edge of the table with the no. 2 script liner.

s t e p **4** · In this step, deepen the shading to enhance the contour of the objects; be sure the middle value separates the dark and light colors or the dimensional effect will not work.

Deepen the shading in the tulips and bowl by floating Honey Brown on the outer edges using the ¼ -inch flat shader. Do the same for the watering can using Graphite. Also, paint two horizontal lines in Grey Sky to suggest a band around the can with the no. 2 script liner. Shade the lines with thinned Graphite. Using the ¼ -inch shader, add deeper shading to the tulip leaves with Black Green. Float Antique Maroon along the edge of the flowerpot with the ½ -inch shader. Using the ¼ -inch shader, deepen the shadows around your strawberries with Black Plum.

Replace your pattern and transfer the strawberry leaves and ivy. Using the ¼ -inch shader, paint partially hidden ivy leaves Black Green and the rest Hauser Dark Green. Paint the strawberry leaves with Avocado.

*s t e p **5** ·* Dilute Burnt Sienna until very watery and transparent. Load a no. 2 round brush with this mixture and loosely brush onto the watering can where rust might form—such as around the rim and nozzle. Finish the ivy by floating Avocado around the edges and highlighting with Reindeer Moss Green.

With the ¼-inch flat shader, finish the strawberry leaves by floating Hauser Dark Green on one edge and Reindeer Moss Green on the other. With the no. 1 round, add a stem to the larger end of a few strawberries with Avocado, shading with Hauser Dark Green. Dilute Reindeer Moss Green until very watery and add veins to all leaves with a no. 5/0 script liner.

Decorate the bowl with a checkerboard trim in Deep Midnight Blue by making a short stroke with the chisel end of a ¼-inch flat shader, so it resembles a square. Connect these squares by the corners along the front of the bowl. When the trim extends around the sides of the bowl, switch to a no. 1 round brush and make the strokes gradually thinner until you reach the edge of the bowl.

Paint two comma strokes in Titanium White, using a no. 1 round, on either side of the bowl following the contour, to suggest reflective light. Highlight the strawberries with this same color and a ¼-inch shader, but soften the edges of the highlight. Strawberries have a bumpier surface than a glass bowl does, so the highlight on the berries is less defined than the sharper one on the bowl.

I included the background in this final step so you could see where the cast shadows fall against the brick. Use the same diluted shadow mixture that you used around the bricks. With a ½-inch flat shader, apply the shadows of the spout and the tulips to the right and a bit lower than the objects themselves. Keep the shadow mixture very light and transparent.

Paint the Radishes & Topiary Still Life

s t e p **1** · Using a ½ -inch shader, block in the topiary pot with Antique Green, the birdhouse and topiary stem with Slate Grey, the trowel with Grey Sky, and the table and trowel handle with Rookwood Red. With the deerfoot stippler, paint the topiary Black Green with soft stippled edges. Follow the instructions for the Strawberries & Ivy Still Life to paint the flowerpots.

s t e p **2** · Shade the topiary pot with Plantation Pine using the ½ -inch flat shader. Drybrush Graphite onto the birdhouse with a ¼ -inch flat shader, making vertical strokes to imitate wood grain. Using a ½ -inch shader, float Graphite under the eaves of the roof. Paint the edge of the wood with the no. 1 round loaded with Graphite where the hole is cut, and paint the hole Soft Black using a ¼ -inch shader. Use a no. 2 script liner to run a line of Graphite along the right side of the topiary stem. Stipple Avocado onto the topiary with the deerfoot stippler. Let the undercoat of Black Green show more on the lower right side of the foliage shape. Using the ½ -inch shader, shade the trowel with Slate Grey, and blend it into the basecoat with a damp brush. Float Black Plum along the right edge of the trowel handle with the ½ -inch shader, and a thin line of it on the left side. Shade the table as directed in the Strawberries & Ivy Still Life.

s t e p **3** · Reposition your pattern and transfer the radishes and leaves detail. Highlight the table and trowel handle with Cherry Red loaded on the ½ -inch shader. With a no. 1 round, add a touch of Hauser Light Green to the upper rim of the topiary pot. Drybrush Grey Sky onto the birdhouse and roof in vertical strokes using the ½ -inch shader to suggest shingles. Paint the left side of the topiary stem Grey Sky. With the ½ -inch scruffy brush, stipple Light Avocado onto the topiary, keeping the color to the upper left section of the foliage. Basecoat the radishes Titanium White. When radishes are dry, add contour by shading with a mixture of Lilac and a touch of Grey Sky loaded on the ¼ -inch flat shader. Paint the radish leaves Avocado.

s t e p **4** · Add deeper shading to the trowel with Neutral Grey on the inside and on the right side of the handle stem. Paint the perch Neutral Grey. Create a deeper shadow inside the flowerpot by painting Antique Maroon on either side of the trowel's handle. Also use this color along the right sides of the pots. Float Black Green on the topiary pot next to the flowerpots and birdhouse. Also float it along the edges of the radish leaves for shading, and down the middle of the leaves for a center vein. Stipple Reindeer Moss Green into the topiary, keeping the color to the upper left of the foliage. Apply Deep Burgundy on the top half of each radish, drybrushing the edges into the Titanium White halfway down.

s t e p **5** · Dilute Burnt Sienna until it's very watery and with the no. 1 round, brush rust stains on the birdhouse's side and roof. Just above them make a dot for a nail head with a mixture of Soft Black and Burnt Sienna. Load a no. 2 script liner with thinned Soft Black and define the cracks in the wood and outline of the roof on the birdhouse. Draw three staggered lines to suggest the crooked edge of the roof shingles. Using the no. 1 round, shade the underside of the perch with Soft Black and highlight the opposite side with Grey Sky. Make a watery solution of Soft Black and use a small round brush to paint a shadow cast by the perch. Remember to make this shadow point slightly downward and to the right as the other shadows will go. Add Black Plum to the large end of the radishes with the no. 1 round, blending it into the Deep Burgundy. Add Titanium White highlights to the trowel and its handle, the radishes, the topiary stem and the rim of the topiary pot using the ¼-inch flat shader. Accent the edges of the radish leaves with a watery mixture of Burnt Sienna and Olde Gold. Add cast shadows with the ½-inch flat, against the brick as described in the Strawberries & Ivy Still Life.

The Final Touches

ADD THE CHECKERBOARD TRIM

If your surface has a molding or pediment, enchance it with a checkerboard for a country flavor. You can choose to use any color for your checkerboard trim, but I used Moss Green to balance the green baseboard. This taping technique gives you a more finished look than the sponged checkerboard.

Basecoat with Ivory Silk or Titanium White, where you would like the checkerboard trim. Let this dry twenty-four hours.

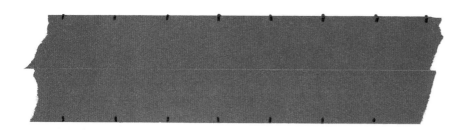

*s t e p **1*** · Apply two strips of 1" wide low-tack painter's tape on top of the basecoat, with the bottom edge of the top strip butting against the top edge of the bottom strip. Mark off 1-inch increments along the tape.

*s t e p **2*** · Use an X-Acto knife to cut the tape vertically along these marks. Take care to press hard enough to cut the tape, but not too hard so that the wood trim is penetrated. A new blade in your knife will give you the best results and require little pressure.

*s t e p **3*** · Pull up every other 1-inch section of tape. Be sure the edges of the remaining pieces are securely adhered, so the paint doesn't seep under them.

*s t e p **4*** · Place another strip of tape along the outside edge to ensure a straight line. Paint each open square with Moss Green using a ½ -inch shader and let dry.

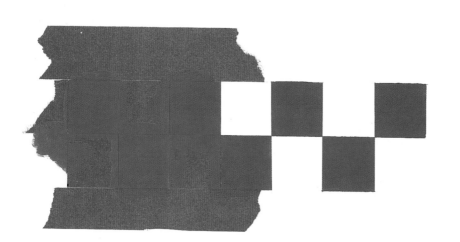

*s t e p **5*** · Carefully remove the re-maining tape by lifting a corner with the tip of an X-Acto knife.

ADD A POETIC LINE

And for a final touch, I used a no. 2 fully loaded script liner to write a poetic line around the opening of the hutch: "The kiss of the sun for pardon, the song of the birds for mirth. One is nearer God's heart in a garden than anywhere else on Earth." I used Glorious Gold, and it was just the right accent when I painted the knobs the same color. When the paint is dry, seal your still lifes and ivy with a coat of water-based polyurethane.

Detail of Poetic Lines, Lattice Work and Checkerboard Trim

Marble-Topped Bird Table

Here's an example of how to recycle furniture. This little end table was left

over from the 1970s and had a drab Early-American maple finish on it.

It was too dated for today's decor, yet it was still a well-built Tell City

product too nice for the trash. It's just the kind of furniture you stash in

the den or spare bedroom, and it makes a perfect candidate for this project.

materials

General Supplies:
- Latex gloves
- Paper towels
- Sea sponge
- Tack cloth
- High-gloss, water-based polyurethane

Brushes:
- nos. 2 and 5/0 script liners
- nos. 0 and 2 round
- ¼" flat shader
- ¼" filbert
- Assorted sponge brushes

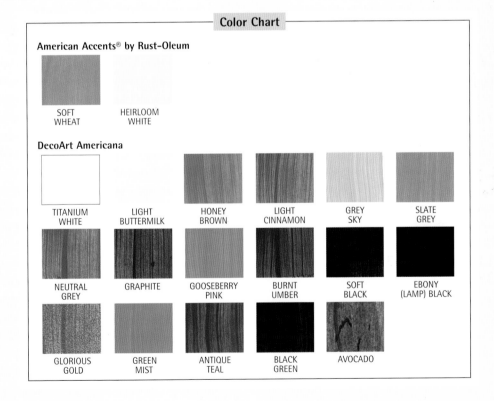

Color Chart

American Accents® by Rust-Oleum

SOFT WHEAT	HEIRLOOM WHITE

DecoArt Americana

TITANIUM WHITE	LIGHT BUTTERMILK	HONEY BROWN	LIGHT CINNAMON	GREY SKY	SLATE GREY
NEUTRAL GREY	GRAPHITE	GOOSEBERRY PINK	BURNT UMBER	SOFT BLACK	EBONY (LAMP) BLACK
GLORIOUS GOLD	GREEN MIST	ANTIQUE TEAL	BLACK GREEN	AVOCADO	

THESE PATTERNS MAY BE HAND-TRACED OR PHOTOCOPIED FOR
PERSONAL USE ONLY. THESE PATTERNS ARE SHOWN FULL SIZE.

Prepare the Surface

Prepare the surface as explained on page 15.
Basecoat your piece in the color of your choice.
Here I used Heirloom White for the cabinet and
Soft Wheat for the door frames.

Easy Faux Marbling

One of the easiest and fastest faux looks is marbling. The trick is in the layering—so if you can dab a sponge, you can marble. This look, along with a couple of classy little songbirds, will lend itself to any surface.

s t e p **1** · Apply one coat of Soft Black with a 2-inch foam brush and let dry. Sand with a brown grocery bag or very fine sand paper; then wipe it clean with a tack cloth. Put on latex gloves. Dampen a sea sponge. Pour a generous amount of Antique Teal onto your palette. Keep several layers of folded paper towels near the palette. Lay the sponge in Antique Teal and blot the excess on the paper towel. Lightly dab the Antique Teal over the Soft Black, rotating the sponge to avoid a repeated pattern and at the same time applying paint diagonally across the surface. The sponged-on paint should be light in coverage and appear grainy. Leave areas of black showing through. Rinse the sponge.

s t e p **2** · Sponge on Green Mist in the same way, allowing previous colors to show through. Maintain a light touch when sponging on paint. Rinse the sponge. Dab Gooseberry Pink on very faintly in a few places to add just a hint of pink. Rinse the sponge.

step **3** · Lightly and *very* sparingly sponge Black Green over the entire surface to add depth.

step **4** · To create veining, load a no. 2 script liner with Light Buttermilk thinned with water. Start at the top and lightly drag the brush diagonally across the surface, twisting the handle in your fingers to make jagged lines. Be sure to follow the same diagonal direction you did when sponging. Lift your brush as you come to the end of a vein, making the lines thinner as they branch out. Accuracy doesn't count here—a shaky hand can make the marbling effect even more natural looking. Remember to stroke in a diagonal direction, and do not cross any lines. Let dry.

Paint the Birds

At first glance a bird can be an intimidating subject to paint. They're so different and their colors and patterns are complex. But if you paint these birds section by section, and one step at a time, it really is a lot easier than it looks.

First of all, be easy on yourself. Don't worry if the color you mix isn't the same shade as pictured. Don't worry if a feather stroke is a bit out of place. These are birds, and thankfully they aren't designed with the lines or perfect angles we artists have to sweat over. As long as you make an accurate tracing of the patterns and use the right brushes for the right job your birds will be stunning.

As a rule, I paint most small things (fruits, florals, small animals) life-size when space allows. Sometimes you can get away with painting things a bit smaller than they normally are, but never make anything larger than life. The patterns for the chickadee and the warbler are both printed life-size in this book. For best results, their size should not be altered.

Center the birds on each door and carefully transfer the patterns.

PAINT THE CHICKADEE

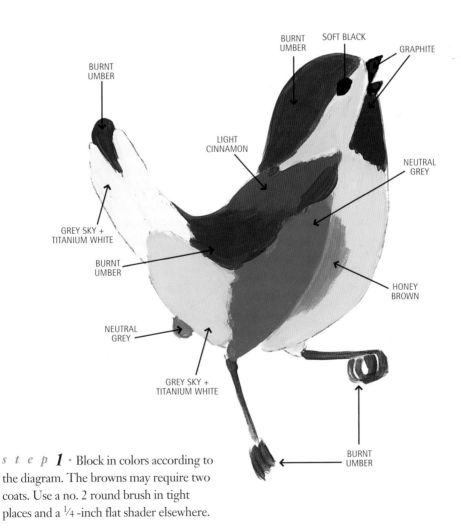

s t e p **1** · Block in colors according to the diagram. The browns may require two coats. Use a no. 2 round brush in tight places and a ¼-inch flat shader elsewhere.

Paint the Birds

TINY STROKES OF SHADING TO CREATE CONTOUR

SOFT BLACK ADDED TO GRAPHITE + DILUTED SHADING HELPS TO DEFINE LAYERS IN WINGS.

TOUCH OF SOFT BLACK ADDED FOR SHAPE

SOFT BLACK ADDED TO DILUTED HONEY BROWN

A TOUCH OF TITANIUM WHITE ADDED TO BURNT UMBER BRINGS OUT THE CONTOUR OF THE HEAD.

DILUTED TITANIM WHITE IS DRYBRUSHED OVER ROUNDED AREAS TO CREATE SHAPE AND DIMENSION.

s t e p **2** · Shade each section of color by mixing the original color with a touch of Soft Black to darken it slightly and water to thin it. Your original color mixture will be used again later, so I suggest you scoop some of the original color onto a stir stick and mix it with the Soft Black on another area of your palette. Then use the no. 2 round brush to apply shading around the edges of the original color. For instance, the "cap" on the chickadee's head is Burnt Umber so when you darken that color with Soft Black and get a deeper brown, use it to shade the Burnt Umber sections only. Add the black sparingly—a little goes a long way. A touch with the end of your bristles will do. You will have to mix a new shade for each color. Once you have painted the shade onto a section, rinse your brush and wet-dab the inner edges to soften and blend.

s t e p **3** · Drybrush the highlights on top of the original colors by mixing Titanium White with the original color to make it lighter. In the darker areas, add Titanium White sparingly, but add more Titanium White over the light gray areas. Be sure to keep your highlights surrounded by the original color—a highlight and shade color should never touch; always keep them separated with the original color. Highlight the upper breast and rump areas, but the lowest part of the belly should remain shaded.

FINAL HIGHLIGHTS OVER THE BROWN AREAS ARE PAINTED WITH HONEY BROWN.

MORE TITANIUM WHITE ADDED TO THE BREAST MAKES THE AREA LOOK FULLER.

HIGHLIGHTED LEGS AND FEET

step **4** · Accentuate the highlighted areas by applying more Titanium White—a little thicker—in the breast and rump areas and below the eye. Use Honey Brown to highlight the high spots on the cap and bird's back. Add deeper gray shading to the belly around the legs by adding a bit of Soft Black to the original Grey Sky/Titanium White mixture. Blend upward with a clean, damp brush. Use this same color, diluted on a no. 0 round brush, to define the scalloped feather lines in the wing and tail feathers. Also apply it lightly to the shaded cheek area. Drybrush Titanium White onto the feathers. Mix Titanium White with Burnt Umber using a no. 0 round brush and run a highlight line along the legs and claws.

step **5** · Add the talons to the ends of the feet with Soft Black, and highlight with a fine line of Titanium White. Outline the eye with Graphite. Add a tiny speck of reflective light on the right side of the eyeball and a small line on the upper beak with Titanium White.

Paint the branch following the directions for the topiary stem in the "Garden Shed Cabinet" project on page 83. Load a ¼ -inch filbert brush with Avocado and drag the side of the bristles through Titanium White. Place the brush at the top of the leaf bud and bring it down toward the stem, turning and lifting the brush so that the stroke ends at a peak. Use this technique for all the buds, working back and forth between the painting and the palette. Various color and shape differences in the buds are just fine—don't try to make each one like the first.

Paint the Birds

PAINT THE WARBLER

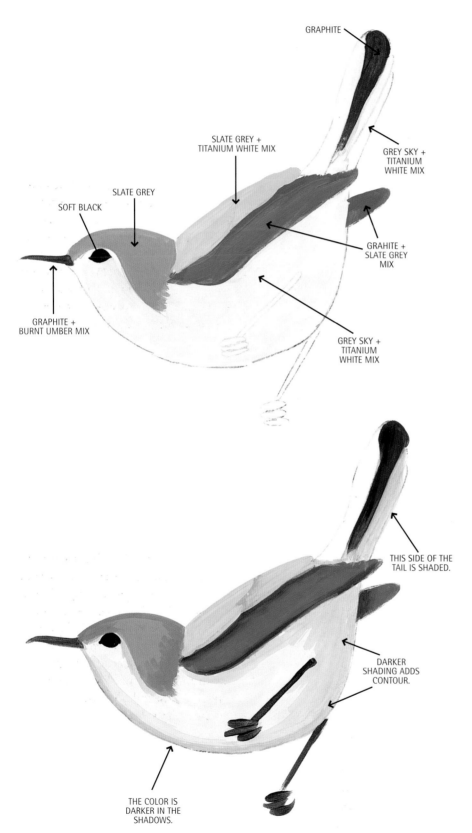

GRAPHITE

SLATE GREY +
TITANIUM WHITE MIX

GREY SKY +
TITANIUM
WHITE MIX

SLATE GREY

SOFT BLACK

GRAHITE +
SLATE GREY
MIX

GRAPHITE +
BURNT UMBER MIX

GREY SKY +
TITANIUM
WHITE MIX

THIS SIDE OF THE
TAIL IS SHADED.

DARKER
SHADING ADDS
CONTOUR.

THE COLOR IS
DARKER IN THE
SHADOWS.

s t e p **1** · Mix the following paint mixtures on your palette: Graphite and Burnt Umber, (1:1); Slate Grey and Titanium White, (1:1); Grey Sky and Titanium White, (2:1); and Graphite and Slate Grey, (1:1). Block in sections of the bird's body as shown. Don't worry about painting over the foot—it will show through the light paint.

s t e p **2** · Add a touch of Soft Black to each of your mixes to get a darker shade. (Note: As before, your original color mixture will be used again later, so create the shading mix on another area of your palette.) Dilute each shade and apply it to the contours of each section, just as you did the Chickadee. Paint the legs with the Graphite/Burnt Umber mix.

CURVED &
STRAIGHT LINES

DILUTED TITANIUM WHITE
LIGHTENS THESE AREAS

s t e p **3** · Mix Titanium White with
your original colors to create a lighter tint,
and highlight according to the diagram.
Add Titanium White to the Graphite and
Slate Grey mixture. Dilute the mix and
load it on a no. 5/0 script liner. "Stripe" the
wings to suggest individual feathers—a bit
curved toward the shoulder and straight
lines down the rest of the wing.

TINY STROKES HELP
SOFTEN HARD LINES.

A SHADOW AT THE
BASE OF THE LEG
PARTS THE FEATHERS.

s t e p **4** · Add the lighter highlights
to the throat and breast area, head and tail.
Highlight the stripes in the wings. With a
small round brush, apply deeper shadows
in the overlap of the wing and where the
head meets the back. Stroke fine lines
around the eye, pointing to the right and
downward. Add feather lines to the tail
and at the base of the leg where it is at-
tached to the body

Paint the Birds

C O N T I N U E D

JUST A HINT OF
HONEY BROWN
UNDER THE WING.

SHARP WHITE HIGHLIGHT
ON BRANCH MAKES IT
COME FORWARD.

LIGHT DOESN'T HIT
THIS WING TIP—
MAKE IT DARKER.

TINY WHITE COMMA
STROKES HIGHLIGHT
THE "WRINKLED" FEET.

s t e p **5** · With a ¼-inch shader,
float Honey Brown on the belly against
the wing. Dilute Graphite and apply it
with the no. 5/0 script liner to the wings
and tail to define the lines. Make fine
strokes around the neck line and eye, and a
few lines in the dark shadow behind the
legs. Shade the bottom of the beak and the
right side of the legs and feet with Soft
Black. Paint fine curved talons onto the
feet. Load the no. 5/0 script liner with diluted Titanium White and paint a ring
around the eye. Highlight the top beak
and apply a speck of light into the eye with
Titanium White. Run Titanium White
down the center left of the legs and feet.

The Final Touches

A sealant is a must if you want your "marble" to look convincing. Two to three light, even coats of high-gloss, water-based polyurethane will add the shine and depth you want. Paint any trim and knobs with Glorious Gold.

The Completed "Marbled" Top

Chickadee and Warbler, detail

Canning Jars Cabinet

This scene was a familiar sight at Grandma's house—shelves full of canned

vegetables that she had put up the prior year. Well, painting these jars is as

close as I'll ever come to this kitchen chore! And painting these two jars—

filled with corn and beets—is a lot easier than it looks. Paint this little

cabinet and bring a touch of Grandma back into your kitchen!

materials

General Supplies:
- Transfer paper
- Clean cotton rags
- Latex gloves
- Americana DecoArt Faux Glazing Medium
- 8 oz. Americana Weathered Wood Crackle Medium
- Carver-Tripp® Safe and Simple™ Wood Stain (Special Walnut)
- Carver-Tripp® Safe and Simple™ Polyurethane (Satin)
- Chalk pencil

Brushes:
- ¼" and ½" flat shader
- nos. 2 and 5/0 script liners
- no. 0 round
- 1" bristle trim brush
- ¼" cat's tongue

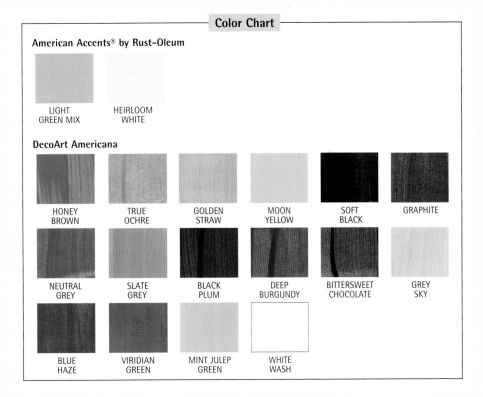

Color Chart

American Accents® by Rust-Oleum

LIGHT GREEN MIX · HEIRLOOM WHITE

DecoArt Americana

HONEY BROWN · TRUE OCHRE · GOLDEN STRAW · MOON YELLOW · SOFT BLACK · GRAPHITE

NEUTRAL GREY · SLATE GREY · BLACK PLUM · DEEP BURGUNDY · BITTERSWEET CHOCOLATE · GREY SKY

BLUE HAZE · VIRIDIAN GREEN · MINT JULEP GREEN · WHITE WASH

THESE PATTERNS MAY BE HAND-TRACED
OR PHOTOCOPIED FOR PERSONAL USE ONLY.
THESE PATTERNS ARE SHOWN FULL SIZE.

Prepare the Surface

Prepare the surface as instructed on page 15. Then stain the entire piece—inside and out—following the directions on the can. Normally, if these are the only areas that will remain stained, I'd take particular care when staining the top of a cabinet and door center. However, since you are doing a crackle technique on this cabinet, the "old" surface will be showing through the cracks, so it is necessary to stain the entire piece. See "Kerry's Crackling Technique" for step-by-step instructions.

After your crackling has dried, mark off 2-inch chalk lines down the center door panel, stopping about three-quarters of the way down to suggest a wainscot-ing effect. Go over these lines with thinned Soft Black, using a no. 2 script liner. On the "shelf" that the jars sit on, create an illusion of depth by drawing your lines horizontally, making them closer together as they recede toward the back wall. Go over your lines with Bittersweet Chocolate loaded onto a no. 2 script liner.

Enlarge the pattern of the jars until the corn jar is 7½ inches tall. Center your pattern so that the bottom of the corn jar is about 1½ to 2 inches below the topmost horizontal line or the back edge of the shelf you painted. Transfer the pattern, omitting the beets and the word "Ball."

Kerry's Crackling Technique

1 Apply crackle medium in the direction of the wood grain with a 1-inch bristle trim brush to the sides, front, drawer front and door frame. Do NOT apply it to the top of the cabinet or the center panel of the door. Allow to dry for about forty-five minutes.

2 Mix approximately 8 parts Moss Green to 1 part Heirloom White to achieve a Light Green Mix. It's kind of a "utensil green" (remember Grandma's utensils with the green wooden handles?) and should match the Mint Julep Green you'll use for the jars.

hint Crackle medium should be shiny when dry. If it isn't, another coat is necessary, but don't apply it too thick.

3 Paint the sides, front, and inside of the door frame with the Light Green Mix. Paint the drawer (make sure the pull is removed) and door frame with Heirloom White.

4 When the drawer is dry, simulate gingham plaid by painting stripes up, down and across the drawer front with the Light Green Mix and a ½ -inch flat shader.

Paint the Canning Jars

s t e p **1** · Using a ½ -inch flat shader, block in the backgrounds—Honey Brown for the corn jar and Black Plum for the beet jar. Paint around the bail so it will be visible later. Paint the metal lid on the corn jar Neutral Grey. Put a dime-size amount of True Ochre on your palette. Hold a piece of paper against the side of the jar to mask and help protect the background. Then, dip the tip of your forefinger into True Ochre, and paint dots of corn all over the Honey Brown base. Dip your finger into the paint often to avoid making fingerprints. Allow plenty of the darker background to show through. Re-position your pattern and transfer the beets. Paint the beets with one coat of Deep Burgundy.

s t e p **2** · Add shading to the metal lid with Graphite applied to the sides and around the rim. Keep the threads on the side curving downward so they follow the shape and are parallel to the lower edge of the lid.

Pour a very small amount of Golden Straw and Moon Yellow onto your palette side by side. Finger paint Golden Straw on top of the corn you already painted, but with this layer, paint to the middle-left of the jar so you will have a concentrated area of lightness to suggest where the light is falling. Then finger paint another layer of corn, this time using Moon Yellow. Paint less corn this time and keep the finger-painted dots within the area you last painted with Golden Straw.

Add another coat of Deep Burgundy to the centers of the beets, and blend the edges so they disappear as they get closer to the outer edge. This second coat will add opacity to the otherwise burgundy pigment and lighten the color. Paint over the bail if you want, since the transparency of the Deep Burgundy allows the bail's shape to remain visible.

s t e p **3** · With a no. 1 round brush, highlight the metal lid with Slate Grey, applying it just to the upper half of each thread, and along the outer rim on the top. Very lightly drybrush over the threads on the side with the same color to soften the depth of the ridges and obscure any smoothness in its appearance—it is an old jar lid so there should be nothing perfect about it.

Add a small amount of Moon Yellow to White Wash and make random U shapes with the no. 0 round brush on top of the lightest finger-painted dots. The open end of the U should be slightly closed, making the corn kernel-shaped. Also make tiny comma strokes that face each other, but aren't connected at the bottom, like this: / \.

Add a touch of White Wash to Deep Burgundy to visibly lighten it. Dab this color into the center-left of each beet with the ¼-inch cat's tongue. Keep the color to the upper-left, because that is where your light source is coming from. Damp-blend this color into the next darker color.

Dilute Mint Julep Green and load it onto the no. 2 script liner. With your brush placed just on the inside of the original outline and on top of the Honey Brown, paint an eighth-inch thick line down the sides and around the bottom of the corn jar, simulating the look of light green glass. When this is dry, mix a 1:1 ratio of Mint Julep Green and Faux Glazing Medium. Float this mixture with the ½-inch flat shader along the line you just painted and under the rim of the lid at the neck of the jar, softening the previous line. Add a touch of Viridian Green to the Mint Julep Green. Using the no. 2 script liner, paint a fine line in the center of the green outline along the bottom of the corn jar and on the right side of the neck to give the illusion of thickness to the green glass.

Mix a 1:1 ratio of Viridian Green and Blue Haze to create a more-green-than-blue tint and outline the beet jar with the script liner as you did the corn jar. Do NOT outline the upper edge of the glass top. Let dry. Mix a 1:1 ratio of this green/blue mixture with Faux Glazing Medium to create a transparent shade. If it is not transparent, add more glazing medium. Using a ½-inch flat shader, paint in the glass lid and neck of the beet jar with this blue/green glaze. Float it down the sides of the jar as you did on the corn jar.

Paint the Canning Jars

s t e p **4** · With the ¼-inch flat shader, highlight the beets with a dot of thinned White Wash damp blended into the darker color. Notice there are a few beets that appear to be above the surface of the liquid at the top of the jar. You can easily create that illusion by painting thin, tiny lines of White Wash about one-quarter of the way down the beets to reflect the light hitting the surface of the liquid.

Dilute White Wash until thin, but not totally transparent. Using the ¼-inch flat shader, pull filmy streaks of reflection down the sides of the corn jar, beginning at the shoulder and following the contour of the glass. Use this same thin white to paint the front edge of the glass lid on the beet jar to add roundness. Add a touch of the blue/green glaze mix to your thinned white. Pull down filmy streaks of light on the beet jar just as you did for the corn jar. With this same color, draw a thin film of light horizontally but not straight across the curved shoulder of the beet jar. In order for it to be visually correct, it must be almost parallel to the raised ridge around the neck.

Load the no. 2 script liner with White Wash, full strength but thinned enough for use in a liner, and pull streaks of reflected light (shorter than the filmy streaks) down the sides of both jars. Curve the streaks of reflection as the glass curves. Concentrate the strongest or whitest reflections at the shoulder of each jar. Pull one or two fine lines down the center of the corn jar. Paint strong light reflections on the ridges of the beet jar using the tip of your liner

brush. The round rings on the glass lid will require small comma strokes of highlight also. Refer back to the picture when in doubt regarding the reflections. Use the no. 0 round to dry brush white highlights onto the lightest areas of the threads on the metal lid. You want this lid to look old, so make sure the highlights are subtle or it will look shiny and new.

Paint the bail Bittersweet Chocolate loaded on the no. 1 round brush. If it is no longer visible, reposition your pattern and transfer it onto the jar. Add a touch of White Wash to the Bittersweet Chocolate and highlight the left side of the top bail and the top of the neck bail. Refer to the picture for the highlight placement. With the no. 1 round, shade the bail on the right and underneath sides with Soft Black. Use the no. 0 round brush loaded with Soft Black to add deeper shadows into the threads of the metal lid of the corn jar, but only on the right side where the shadow would be darkest.

Reposition the pattern and transfer the "Ball" logo onto the beet jar. Load the no. 5/0 script liner with the green/blue mix and go over the lines lightly. Rinse your brush and load with White Wash, painting thin highlights along the left side of the darker lines, but only where the lines are curved. In other words, imagine where the light would reflect off the raised letters and paint accordingly. If in doubt, refer back to the picture. Add shadows as directed in "The Garden Shed Cabinet" project, page 82.

Add the Final Touches

After your finished painting is completely dry, apply a thin coat of water-based polyurethane with a 2-inch sponge brush.

Add the Apple

* Transfer the apple pattern onto your surface, turning the apple so it lies like the one in the photo and is lower than either of the jars since it is closer to the foreground. Paint it according to the instructions in Project 3. Add shadows as directed in Project 5, page 82.

Bunny Hutch

You can make almost any piece of furniture into a Bunny Hutch as long as

it has a suitable flat door or panel. Kitchen cabinets, jelly cupboards and

Hoosiers are excellent country pieces on which to work. This 1930s kitchen

cabinet is an ideal piece because the best visual effects are achieved when this

technique is painted on doors with a raised molding that has been finished

beforehand. But don't let it intimidate you; you can paint one door or all of

them—it's your project. And here are two bunnies to whet your appetite, along

with the complete instructions for painting chicken wire that will fool the eye.

materials

General Supplies
- Chalk Pencil
- Transfer Paper
- Latex gloves
- Paper towels
- Toothpicks
- Water-based polyurethane

Brushes
- ¼", ½" and 1" flat shader
- nos. 2 and 5/0 script liner
- ½" rake brush
- nos. 0 and 2 round
- ¹/₄" deerfoot stippler

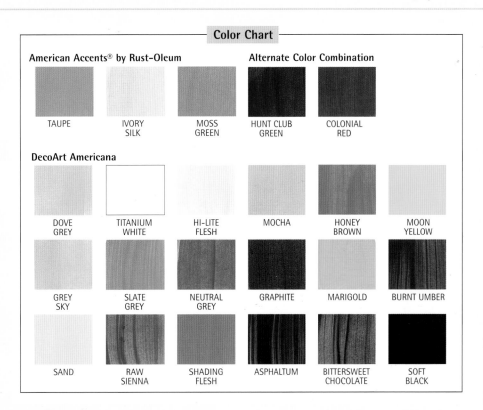

Color Chart

American Accents® by Rust-Oleum

TAUPE · IVORY SILK · MOSS GREEN

Alternate Color Combination

HUNT CLUB GREEN · COLONIAL RED

DecoArt Americana

DOVE GREY · TITANIUM WHITE · HI-LITE FLESH · MOCHA · HONEY BROWN · MOON YELLOW

GREY SKY · SLATE GREY · NEUTRAL GREY · GRAPHITE · MARIGOLD · BURNT UMBER

SAND · RAW SIENNA · SHADING FLESH · ASPHALTUM · BITTERSWEET CHOCOLATE · SOFT BLACK

Carrot

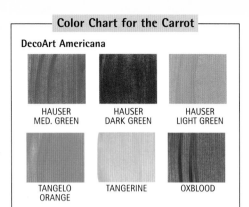

Color Chart for the Carrot

DecoArt Americana

HAUSER MED. GREEN	HAUSER DARK GREEN	HAUSER LIGHT GREEN
TANGELO ORANGE	TANGERINE	OXBLOOD

THIS PATTERN IS FULL SIZE AND MAY BE HAND-TRACED OR PHOTOCOPIED FOR PERSONAL USE ONLY.

Grey Rex Rabbit

Dwarf Lop Rabbit

Chicken Wire Stencil

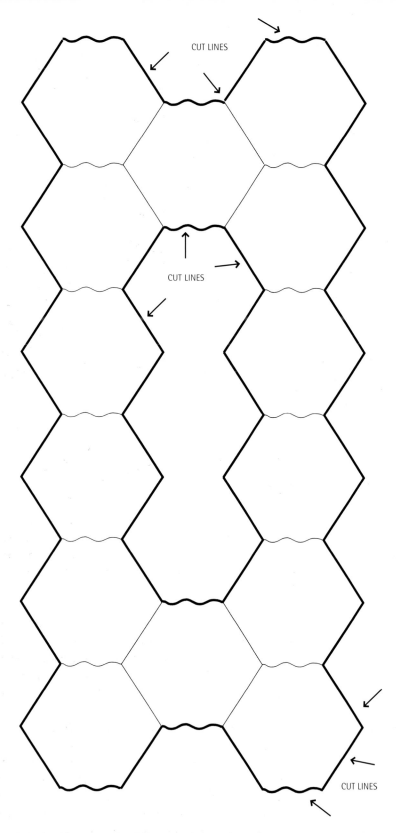

CUT LINES

CUT LINES

CUT LINES

Prepare the Surface

Prepare the surface as instructed on page 15. Remove the doors and hardware. Place each door on an easel, if possible. Paint the background of the doors the same color as the cabinet. Here they are painted Taupe and the clapboard back wall is simulated by painting vertical Graphite lines. Transfer the pattern onto the door with transfer paper. Taupe allows for the use of either black or white transfer paper. Since the rabbit will be nestled in a bed of straw, be sure to allow at least two inches between the bottom of the rabbit and the frame at the bottom of the door.

Paint the Grey Rex Bunny

step **1** · Paint the area from the bottom of the rabbit to the edges of the door Soft Black, creating the base in which you will later paint the straw. At the top of this black area, where it meets the back wall, paint blades of straw in Soft Black by pulling quick, upward strokes about two inches high with a no. 2 liner brush.

> *hint*   If painting more than one panel or door, paint all of the background and straw at the same time. When painting two doors that hang side-by-side, be sure the straw stays at the same level on each door. The rabbits will be painted individually.

Block in colors with a ½ -inch flat shader using Neutral Grey for the body and ears, and Graphite on the face, inside of the ear and front paws. Load a ½ -inch rake brush with Neutral Grey and blot once on a paper towel.

> *hint*   When using the rake brush, the full effect of the specially designed bristles are not achieved if the paint is not thin enough.

Pull short, soft strokes outward around the outer edge of the bunny's fur, and even shorter strokes coming off the ears. Keep in mind that a bunny's coat lays down, so make your strokes in the growth direction and not sticking straight out. Rinse the brush and load it with thinned Graphite and soften the hair line between the Graphite and Neutral Grey by stroking from the Graphite area outward–making the Graphite hair overlap the Neutral Grey hair. Fill in the eye with Soft Black.

step **2** · With a ½ -inch flat shader, float Soft Black around the contour of the face. Deepen the shadow inside the ear with black, and soften the edge with a damp brush. Paint a line around the contour of the front foot where it overlaps the back one using the edge of the ½ -inch flat shader. With the rake brush, stroke on darker fur around the neck and bottom edge of the rabbit, using thinned Graphite. Stroke darker tufts of fur at the base of the left ear, and shade the ear in back to help separate the two.

Then, paint in the first layer of straw by making bold Xs and random strokes of Honey Brown using the no. 2 liner brush. Make them all over the black area, under and around the bunny. Allow some straw to overlap his foot. Paint the blades of straw up to the shadows previously painted in black, but do not cover them completely.

Paint the Grey Rex Bunny

s t e p **3** · Dilute a few drops of Neutral Grey mixed with Slate Grey until it is the consistency of ink. With the rake brush, make light, short strokes over the Neutral Grey areas.

> *h i n t*   Keep the paint thin enough to avoid a dry-brush look, but not enough to appear translucent.

This technique will texturize the surface and help make it look more like hair. Refer to the finished picture to check the direction of hair growth.

Apply Neutral Grey to texturize the Graphite area using the same brushstroke. Concentrate a few strokes over the eye to create a brow and a few lines above the mouth. Use the rake brush to make the lighter hair appear to overlap the darker hair. Dot this by stroking the lighter Neutral Grey into the darker areas. The places that show overlapped hair would be where the jowl area overlaps the neck, where the chest hair overlaps the neck, where the chest hair overlaps the front feet, and on the right ear where the tufts of hair overlap the inside of the ear and the background ear. Add another layer of straw using Marigold. Use the same strokes as before, and allow some of the blades of straw to come up in front of the rabbit.

s t e p **4** · Mix a touch of Soft Black into the Graphite and add deep shadows on the neck and base of the ear. Define the V shape of the nose and add darker strokes over the eye and into the brow. Dilute Grey Sky with water and load on the rake brush. Add lighter strokes of highlight onto the face behind the eye, on the front edges of the ears, on the chest, and on the upper shoulder area. Add a few strokes around the nose and cheek area to help define the contour. Add a touch of Titanium White to the diluted Grey Sky and load it onto a no. 5/0 script liner. Using quick, outward strokes, paint whiskers emerging from the cheek and above the eye. The whiskers are slightly curved downward and tapered to a fine point.

Apply the last layer of straw using the same stroke as before and Moon Yellow. Toward the lower part of the straw, add a few Titanium White highlights to some of the Moon Yellow strokes. The bunny should look nestled in the straw—not sitting on top of it. Paint more strokes of straw in Honey Brown and Marigold in front of the bunny's body to correct this problem.

Paint the Bunny Eyes

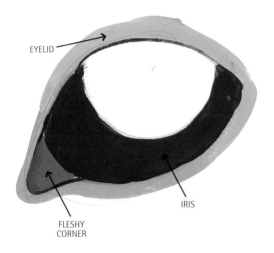

EYELID

FLESHY
CORNER

IRIS

s t e p **1** · Using a no. 1 round, paint the iris Asphaltum. Mix Shading Flesh and Slate Grey to create mauve. Paint the corner of the eye with this shade and add a small amount of Titanium White to the mix to paint the outer rim.

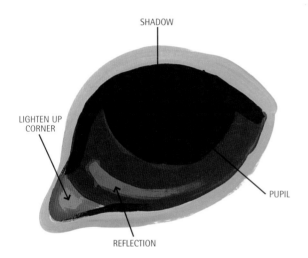

SHADOW

LIGHTEN UP
CORNER

REFLECTION

PUPIL

s t e p **2** · Highlight the corner of the eye by painting this same lighter mauve in the center of the darker color with the no. 1 round. Using a no. 0 round, paint the pupil and inside upper lid Soft Black. Add a touch of Titanium White to the Asphaltum to lighten it only slightly. Using a no. 0 round brush, paint an upside-down comma stroke in the iris near the lower lid, simulating a slight reflection.

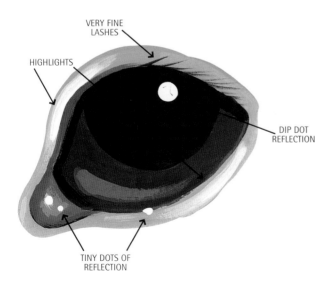

VERY FINE
LASHES

HIGHLIGHTS

DIP DOT
REFLECTION

TINY DOTS OF
REFLECTION

s t e p **3** · Add more Titanium White to the mauve mix and highlight the arch of each eyelid with a no. 0 round. Dip the end of a toothpick into White Wash and make a dip-dot reflection in the near center of the pupil. Make one or two tiny dots of Titanium White in the corner of the eye. Load Titanium White onto a no. 2 round brush and make a sharp point with the bristles. Then, stroke a tiny reflection on the bottom eyelid where the lid meets the eyeball. Load the no. 5/0 script liner with diluted Asphaltum and stroke out a few fine eyelashes on the top eyelid.

Paint the Dwarf Lop Bunny

s t e p **1** · Mix a 1:1 ratio of Mocha and Sand. Basecoat the bunny and let dry. Reposition your pattern and tracing paper to transfer the inside lines of the rabbit. Add a touch of Raw Sienna to the basecoat color, enough to darken it slightly and drybrush it into areas of the rabbit that are shaded, primarily on the right side of the face and around the contours of the body. Don't be too precise here. It will be obscured by more strokes later. Your main concern is to shade appropriate areas and dry brush in the direction of the hair growth.

s t e p **2** · Thin Raw Sienna for use on the rake brush. Load the rake brush and blot once onto a paper towel. Cover the rabbit with tiny strokes of "hair," taking care to make your strokes follow the direction of the hair's natural growth. Reload the rake brush often and add water to your paint if it becomes too thick to flow freely from the bristles. Concentrate more color in areas that require more shading. Thin Burnt Umber as you did the Raw Sienna. Apply deeper shading to areas that require it—under the ears and wherever there are crevices or folds in the coat. Paint straw as instructed on page 113-114.

s t e p **3** · Highlight areas of the bunny's coat with thin Hi-Lite Flesh loaded on the rake brush. A heavier concentration of strokes should be applied to the edge of the left ear where it seems to catch more light. Use this same color and brush to paint the tail, making strokes go from the base of the tail upward and out.

s t e p **4** · Use thinned Bittersweet Chocolate for the darkest shadows, applied with a ¼-inch flat shader on the right side of the face, under the chin, on the side in front of his foot, and in the shadow of the left ear. Use what's left in the brush to drybrush the contour of the cheeks. Use full-strength Bittersweet Chocolate on a no. 5/0 script liner to draw a fine line in the darkest shadow to suggest the edge of each ear against the body. Using the same color, define the V in the nose, make a tiny line for a mouth, and pull out tiny lashes above the eyes. Paint the eyes as directed on page 115. Highlight the area around the nose with Hi-Lite Flesh and no. 0 round brush. Add whiskers as directed for the Grey Rex Bunny. Add a shadow to the back wall and finish the straw as instructed on page 114.

The Chicken Wire

When the rabbit is complete and you have sufficient straw around him, it's time to apply the chicken wire. Make sure you are happy with the painting, as there is no changing it once the chicken wire is painted. By following these simple steps, you will create an illusion that will truly fool the eye.

● TRANSFER THE CHICKEN WIRE

s t e p **1** · Transfer the chicken wire stencil shown on page 112 to card stock or poster board. Carefully cut along the outside edge (bold lines) of the template with an X-Acto knife and straightedge. Do not cut individual "honeycombs" apart. (For the sake of clarity, I will refer to each 6-sided unit of chicken wire as a "honeycomb.")

s t e p **2** · Place the template lengthwise against the upper-left edge of the door frame (the squiggly lines must be vertical). If your door does not have a frame that would act as a level, you must use a square or leveling aid to make sure the stencil is applied correctly.

Trace around all edges of the template with your pencil. (Note: If your background is dark, a white chalk pencil well-sharpened works best; otherwise a no. 2 graphite pencil may be used.) Move the template across the door and line it up with the end of the first tracing. Continue tracing around the template until you have completed three rows of chicken wire. Don't worry about the twisted vertical wire at this time. Move the template down to make three more rows, and fit the template into the bottom of the first section of chicken wire, making a staggered pattern. Simply move the template over to trace individual "honeycombs" that have been skipped by the staggered stacking of the template. When you begin tracing over areas of the bunny itself, switch to a lighter

or darker pencil to ensure your marks will show up against the changing background colors. It is frustrating later when you are painting the wire and cannot see your pencil lines.

Continue tracing around the template until the entire door is covered. At this

time you may fill in the vertical twisted wire with the pencil, but it is just as easy to do it later with the paintbrush and save yourself an unnecessary step.

PAINT THE CHICKEN WIRE

Paint the wire from the top of the door, one row at a time and from left to right with a no. 5/0 script liner. Remember, skinny bristles need skinny paint, so thin your paint well! When you load your brush make sure you work it to a nice point on your palette.

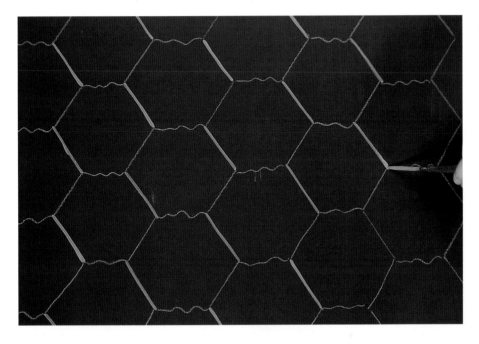

step 1 · Turn your work to make painting more comfortable. Dilute Slate Grey and paint all the wires on the upper-right edge of each honeycomb, provided you turned your work as you see here.

step 2 · With your work still turned to a comfortable painting position, dilute Grey Sky and assuming your light source is in the upper right, paint the upper-left wires, provided you turned your work as you see here. Using the same color, paint a thin, curvy line from the bottom point of one honeycomb to the top point of the one directly below it. Make a slight squiggly line to suggest that the wire is twisted. This technique is best achieved when the stroke is pulled toward you and you wiggle your wrist slightly. Don't worry about imperfect lines. The most important part is maintaining a fine line and not letting strokes end past the point where two wires meet.

The Chicken Wire

step 3 · Highlight areas of the chicken wire randomly with thin strokes of Titanium White where the light would hit the wire. Paint two or three tiny comma strokes of white on the twisted wire to make it look convincing.

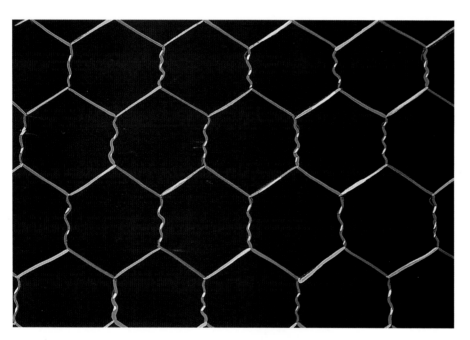

step 4 · To create the illusion of space between the wire and the rabbit, it will help to remember that dark colors recede and light colors come forward. If you find that any of your wire has completely blended into the color of the rabbit behind it, don't be concerned. This is bound to happen when painting a grey bunny. For instance, if the Slate Grey chicken wire is painted over areas of the same color in the bunny's fur, either lighten or darken the wire to add contrast and in turn put depth between the chicken wire and the rabbit.

Adding the Rest of the Straw

Your final strokes to the doors are to add a bit of whimsy. Paint a few random blades of straw around the outer edge of the cage where straw might poke out and hang over the door frame. Don't get carried away with these strokes—four or five will do. To make these blades look especially dimensional, paint them Marigold, then highlight the upper edge with Moon Yellow, and the shaded underside with Honey Brown. Paint shadows that would be cast on the door frame by the straw sticking out of the cage. Spacing the shadows about ½-inch below and at a 45° angle from the blade helps to add dimension.

Add the Carrot

No bunny hutch is complete without a carrot. Paint this little surprise onto the back wall of a shelf or the inside of a drawer.

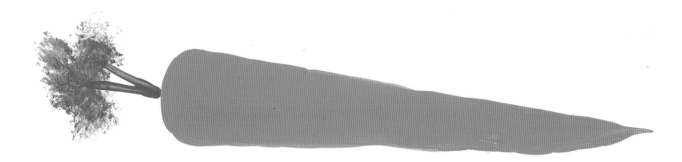

s t e p **1** · Using a ¼-inch flat shader, paint the carrot with two coats of Tangelo Orange. Paint the stem with the shader loaded with Hauser Medium Green, and pounce the foliage on with the deerfoot stippler or scruffy brush.

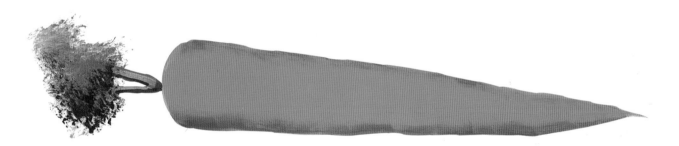

s t e p **2** · Float Oxblood along the edges of the carrot with the ¼-inch shader. Shade the stem using a no. 0 round loaded with Hauser Dark Green, and stipple the same color on lower part of foliage with the deerfoot stippler or scruffy brush.

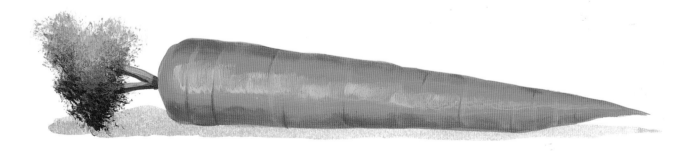

s t e p **3** · With the ¼-inch shader, run Tangerine down the center of the carrot to highlight. Make wrinkles around the carrot by using a no. 0 brush and Oxblood, then highlight the wrinkles with Tangerine. Stipple Hauser Light Green on the upper portion of the foliage, and along the upper edges of the stem.

The Final Touches

After the panels are painted, allow to dry thoroughly before applying one coat of water-based polyurethane with the 2" foam brush. It is not necessary to apply polyurethane over latex paint so use a no. 2 round brush to apply the polyurethane over the straw sticking out of the cage.

> *hint* If small bubbles appear in the polyurethane from the foam brush, gently blow on them before they dry and they will disappear.

Let dry for two hours before re-hanging the door.

Paint the drawer pulls and any trim Moss Green, if desired. Replace hardware and re-hang doors. Replace pulls when dry. Finish the cabinet by using any of the aging techniques shown in the front of this book.

Seed Packet Plaque

Chicken Cupboard

Hens Dry Sink

Faux Delft Tile Dry Sink

Detail of the barn

Detail of the house

Craft Catalog (brushes)
P. O. Box 1069
Reynoldsburg, OH 43068
1-800-777-1442

DecoArt™
P. O. Box 360
Stanford, KY 40484
1-800-367-3047

Déjà Vu Antiques & Collectibles
1060 East Main St.
Brownsburg, IN 46112
317-858-1961

Mastercraft Furniture
S.J. Bailey & Sons, Inc.
P. O. Box 239
Clarks Summit, PA 18411

Rust-Oleum Corporation
11 Hawthorn Pkwy
Vernon Hills, IL 60061

Index